745

A Memoir of World War II

Carl F. Heintze

745 — A Memoir of World War II

© 2014 by Carl F. Heintze

ISBN: 978-1-61170-168-5

Library of Congress Number: 2014936545

745 is based on true events.

All rights reserved. No part of this book may be reproduced, stored in a retrieval system or transmitted in any form or by any means, electronic, mechanical, photocopies, recording or otherwise, without the prior written consent of the author.

Printed in the USA and UK on acid-free paper.

 Robertson Publishing™
www.RobertsonPublishing.com

To order additional copies of this book or any of the following titles visit **www.rp–author.com/Heintze**

> Selected Poems 1940-1990
> Going Home *(A Novel)*
> Two on Two *(Two Novellas)*
> Crush and Heat *(Two stories of the Napa Valley)*
> All They Had *(Stories of War and It's Aftermath)*
> An Island in the Turquoise Sea *(Stories of Kauai)*

Other books by Carl F. Heintze:

A Million Locks and Keys
The Bottom of the Sea and Beyond
The Circle of Fire
The Priceless Pump
Genetic Engineering

Summit Lake
The Forest
Search Among the Stars
The Biosphere
Medical Ethics

IN MEMORY OF DONALD MARSHALL

In the Dictionary of Military Occupations
the code number is 745.
It stands for rifleman, basic.

His job is to close with the enemy,
to kill capture or wound him and
to take his ground.

FOREWORD

This is a personal recollection. I make no apologies for it. It is not meant to be profound, although war is a profound event. It does not attempt to salvage from conflict any universal meaning, although war is filled with universal meanings.

This is a chronicle written eight years after it happened, when memory has grown clouded and parts of the experience are no longer distinct.

It was written with the advantage of both time and life, which should have placed war in a more proper perspective. But time and life have made this chronicle suffer from my inability to transfer the intensity of feeling, which would have made it more real.

Everything in this book is true, insofar as I have been able to remember the truth. But I have been unable to recall the names of many of the men I knew then and there are gaps in my memory of events, especially toward the end of the fighting.

Except where I have had something adverse to say of someone, I have used real names.

Viewed in the cooler light of peace what happened to me was unexceptional. I was only one of many millions. As to all of those other millions, however, my story was important to me. I cannot escape this. It is my defense for the first person singular.

Iwant to write about the war, because in training and fighting and being wounded, I believe I came to manhood. We are often reluctant to write of this passage to maturity in America, but it happens.

I was only four years old when my father died. I never really knew him. The only memories I have are of his last illness: a walk across a mountain town to stay at a friend's house; a hurried call to return home; a long night train journey to Sacramento; one last look as he was wheeled away to the hospital, and my mother's sudden tears after he died.

I grew up without a father, and, although my mother tried to be both a mother and father to me, she could not, of course, completely succeed. As a boy, I was fat, slow and sleepy. When I was 14, I began to wear glasses, and in high school, sports were my terror. I was a failure at all of them.

While other boys played football, or went fishing, or talked of automobiles; I read books and dreamed and wrote bad short stories and worse, poetry. Although I became proficient enough in athletics in college, my boyhood often made me feel different and apart in many ways.

When the war came, I was eager to get into a uniform. I wanted to follow the common rush to service, yet I was afraid I would again be a failure. This conviction was abetted by a long and frustrating attempt to get into the Army.

I tried to enlist twice. Both times I was rejected because I was over the weight limit. The third time I was rejected by my draft board, and for six months I was classified as unfit even to be drafted.

Most of my friends either left home or college due to the war. Finally, after a year of misery, I was accepted for limited service. On September 2, 1943, I was sworn into the Army of the United States.

—Carl Heintze

745

A Memoir of World War II

1

As unhappy as I had been as a civilian, I was even unhappier after a few weeks in the Army. I was sent to the Presidio of Monterey, an induction station. There draftees were fitted with uniforms, given inoculations, interviewed for jobs which they seldom got and then shipped out in carload lots to various camps in the United States for basic training.

It was a strange military establishment. No one carried guns, except the post MP's. The only formations were retreat and reveille and almost everyone had an ailment of some sort.

Most of these were accompanied by long tales of discontent and disgust. Many of the men stationed at Monterey were married and older. They brought their wives to live with them and so instead of being a way of life for them, the Army turned into a job and an inconvenience.

After I had been in the permanent party for a little while — as the troops permanently stationed at the Presidio were called — I was assigned to basic training. This consisted of half a day of the rudiments in the manual of arms, close order drills and a sort of weak-kneed infantry training which was taught to us by a little lieutenant (also limited service) who had been a reserve officer.

In the mornings a platoon of us hiked around the hill upon which the Presidio is built and played like boys at games in the woods of the Del Monte Forest. It was all very harmless and not unlike a Boy Scout camp.

In the afternoons we worked at our various chores about the induction station. I was assigned to the clothing warehouse. I certainly had no qualifications for the job, but I was probably as well fitted for this as anything else I might have been given to do. I disliked it extremely.

Before long I began to feel that the war would pass me by completely, and that, although I was at least in uniform, I was stuck in a most inglorious branch of the service.

The chief difficulty at Monterey was that one simply did not feel he was in the Army. It was a dead backwash of the war, and I can only remember the nine months I spent there as an awful calm, a state of suspension, while I waited for something to happen to me.

Nothing did until the spring of 1944 when I was finally reclassified into general service. The Ninth Service Command, which had control of the Presidio's troops, was being stripped of all able-bodied men. This had been made necessary because of heavy infantry casualties in Euro-c and the Pacific.

In June, 1944, after nine months of playing at being a soldier, I was transferred to the 78th Infantry Division, recently moved to Camp Pickett, Virginia.

2

Virginia in June is hot, and it was hot the day I arrived at Pickett, a raw collection of barracks raked out of the piney woods near Blackstone. When I arrived, I thought I was going to the division quartermaster company. This seemed logical enough since I had been working in a clothing warehouse.

But it only revealed how much I had still to learn about the Army. We were met at the railroad station (I had come across the country with another unfortunate from Monterey) by a truck from the division quartermaster company.

But instead of going to the warehouses, we were sent to the 2nd Battalion, 310th Infantry, one of the regiments of the 78th Division.

It was a Sunday, one of the more disheartening days of my life. After being turned over to a charge of quarters at battalion headquarters, we were taken to temporary billets with F Company.

The few men who were around the barracks set up a long story of complaint as soon as we dropped our two barracks bags on the floor beside our bunks. They kept it up all afternoon. By evening, as other men began to return from passes, the chorus grew until I was sure I had landed in the worst camp in the United States.

The colonel was mad, they said. The non-coms were tyrants. The food was poor and there was not enough of it. The marches were inhuman and the stockade a purgatory. The commanding general was growing fat and rich on a private bus line which he operated to Richmond.

Perhaps the most frightening of all these various soul-crushers—to me, at least—was the harrowing descriptions of physical training and the long marches. Every morning before breakfast the entire division went for a 15-minute "run." No one was allowed to miss it and no one was allowed to fall out.

Marches were just as bad, they said. I was sure that I would never be able to finish even the first one. I went to bed that night sick, scared and wishing that I was back in Monterey.

During the next few weeks, I discovered that the rumors—like most Army rumors—had some truth in them. Pickett was a "hot" camp. The division had recently arrived in Virginia from Camp Butner, North Carolina. All of its privates and privates, first class had been shipped overseas as replacements, leaving only the division cadre and officers and staff.

Two thousand Army Specialized Training Corps men from New England and Middle Atlantic Coastal states had been sent to fill up the ranks. They had been joined by 1500 men from service commands. I was part of a second group of cast-offs scraped up from all over the United States.

This accounted for some of the bitching. The ASTP men resented taking orders from non-coms who had never reached the fourth grade. The non-comns did not like the ASTP men. The service commandos fitted into neither group and like service command men everywhere, they were unhappy. They did not believe they should be in the Army in the first place.

I was an exception to this maxim. The work was hard, the hours were long, the weather was awful, especially to one born and raised in California, but I liked it.

It was what I had come for.

It was over almost before it began. The division did not have time to toughen us. The original ASTP men received eight weeks of refresher training and were already on company problems. The first group of service command men had five weeks of the same routine, and we got only three more before we went on to advanced training.

Our graduation ceremony was a 12 mile march, at night. I faced it with considerable fear, but a vow that I would not fall out. I might collapse from exhaustion in my tracks, but I would never drop beside the road.

We began to hike at parade cadence and in the first hour we covered at least four miles. To my surprise I was still standing when we finished, although many other men had quit. I was able to march back into camp at midnight, too, footsore, but with a confidence in myself that I had never had before. After that I never fell out of a march either in training or combat.

In August the 310th Regiment moved by truck to A.P. Hill Military Reservation near Washington for a series of field problems. It was our first taste of life in the field. We endured attacks of chiggers, mosquitoes and downpours of rain, slept on the ground, sweated profusely and became soldiers.

Then in the midst of training, the division was asked again to provide 1500 privates and privates first class for overseas shipment. I was one of those selected.

3

September 11, 1944. We sailed from New York Harbor aboard the French liner Ile de France, almost a regiment of us. We had no other name than GJ-350 (a). This was our "packet" number, the envelope in which our orders were carried. All of us, even our officers, were replacements being sent to fill gaps in units already overseas.

We had no idea where we were going or how long we would remain together. We had been organized into companies at Fort Meade, Maryland, assigned a company commander, an executive officer and four platoon leaders, given two boxes in which to keep our records and individually saddled with a duffle bag (which we left in France), a huge cargo pack (which we left at the company kitchens and never saw again), a gas mask (which we left somewhere along the road to victory), impregnated clothing for protection against gas (which we never used); a shelter half and several changes of clothing, a mess kit, a helmet and liner, a wool knit cap; and several other items, most of which never got to the front. We were not given rifles.

Staggering under this load, A Company (of which I was company clerk) and B Company boarded an Army ferry at Orangeberg on September 9 and cruised down the Hudson River to the Port of Embarkation pier at 42nd Street, We were the guard companies and so we were the first aboard ship.

For two nights we watched the boats pass on the river, looked at the dock and the houses on the New Jersey shore and explored the Ile de France. On the second day the rest of the troops began to come aboard. By the time we sailed, there were 12,000 of us, sleeping in bunks, four tiers high, and standing in patient lines for everything, including the physical necessities of life.

The Ile de France was fast enough to travel without an escort. It roved in a zig-zag course across the Atlantic. Each morning the monotony was relieved by boat drill when all 12,000 of us raced to the open weather decks, looked at the sea and then reluctantly went below. After 7:30 at night all open decks were closed to troops. Then the latrines were the only places were smoking was allowed and these quickly became the principal meeting places, choked with a gray haze of cigarette smoke and jammed with men.

Our company was led by a captain named Boswell, who looked like a gentle college professor. The executive officer was a huge Southerner named Jackson and our platoon leader was Lieutenant Baker, a fragile youth who did not appear to be more than 18.

The voyage was uneventful. The sun shone, the sea was calm and no submarines came near us — or if they did we never heard about them — and we had nothing to do but stand guard. I was spared even this chore because I was company clerk.

The complaint was the food. It was terrible. It was prepared from British rations by British cooks. Only two meals a day were served, one of which was invariably two soft boiled eggs, two greasy strips of salt pork and two large chunks of white bread. Only the bread and great quantities of orange marmalade kept us going. The beverage served with this conglomerate was supposed to be coffee, but it was an English version and horrible to taste.

Despite this, and the crowding, it was a pleasant voyage and over too soon. On the seventh day we picked up two destroyer escorts and rounded the southern tip of Ireland and the following morning we eased past the submarine boom into the Firth of Clyde and anchored.

4

It was two days before the ship was completely unloaded, since troops could only be taken off in lighters. We were the last to leave. While we waited, we had our first look at Europe – the low green mountains of Scotland – and for the first time we felt that this was truly a great adventure. We had no responsibility and we had no reason to reflect on what lay ahead. Reflection had been destroyed by the swift succession of events and it was necessary to live only from one moment to the next.

The banks of the Firth were dotted with stone houses and the bay itself was full of ships of all kinds. One of these, some sort of a ferry boat, called for us on the afternoon of the second day. Bowed beneath our packs, overcoats and duffle bags, we stood on its deck as it took us to a landing only a short distance from a railroad siding.

In a short time we walked from the landing to the train to the music of a British military band. Women from the Scottish Red Cross were waiting for us with long white hospital pitchers full of coffee.

Then the train began to move and as evening closed in, we sped south through Scotland toward the English border. All along the way as long as it was daylight we stood at the train windows, waving to people in towns. We stopped only once – in Carlylse – and then went steadily south into the blackout and England.

Six of us had been assigned to each compartment, which made sleeping difficult so another man and I went back to the last car, a sort of combination baggage and passenger car, and lay down on the officers' luggage

9

and the record boxes. But we could not sleep. It was too cold and we were too excited.

At midnight we passed through London, completely blacked out and cringing under V-1 and V-2 bombs, and when dawn came, we were coasting into the dock area at Southampton. Quickly we marched into the port, still sealed off to most civilians, and sat down in a big shed to wait for a ship to take us to France.

It docked that afternoon, the *Princess Astrid*, a small Belgian Channel steamer which had been captured by the British at the beginning of the war. Without the usual Army delay, we boarded her — two companies of us — and moved out into the Southampton Roads. Next morning, we were off Omaha Beach, waiting for the fog to lift. As it drifted out to sea and melted into a bright haze in the sunlight, we saw beyond it the high bluffs of France, incredibly cluttered with the debris of war.

In the water about us were many ships, most of them LST's, Liberties or Victories, discharging their cargoes into smaller craft to be taken onto the beach. Barrage balloons still hung over the area and a row of sunken vessels made a breakwater to shield landing craft and DUCK's from the heavier swell of the English Channel.

The *Princess Astrid* coasted slowly in toward the beach, for fear its propeller might churn up a vagrant mine. The water was still filled with the remains of D-Day, although it was now September 29th, more than three months after the big assault. Broken bits of boxes, life jackets, K-ration boxes, belts and other pieces of equipment floated by. Among the debris we saw our first dead man.

He floated past the ship, bloated and face down in the water, his brown uniform puffed full of air, while we crowded to the rail to watch curiously. In a few moments he was gone, and we half wondered if we had really seen him at all.

The *Princess Astrid* carried six landing craft on its already overcrowded deck. They were lowered to deck level and a platoon at a time, we climbed aboard, weighted down again with overcoats, packs and duffle bags. Once in the landing barges, it was almost impossible to move, and we jostled together like sardines in a can as we moved through the low swells to the beach.

The barges were run up on a Mulberry dock at the point where the First Division had landed so tragically on D-Day, and we walked out through the opened ramps. Our first sight was a huge sign proclaiming the area as "Smith Beach" in honor of a colonel of the 16th Infantry who had been killed on D-Day.

We marched up the shingle past a ruined German pillbox and then began to climb slowly up the steep cliff on steps fashioned in the soft earth. It was a hard climb and before we had reached the top, we were sweating and out of breath. To our right was a long shallow ravine, one of the exits from the beach, and on its farther slope we saw rows of white crosses, the first American military cemetery we had seen. It was hardly a welcome sight to a group of infantry replacements.

Soon we were moving through the square hedgerowed fields which are a trade mark of Normandy, then through a wrecked village and finally through a group of pyramidal tents in which rested other replacements. We did not stop here though, but marched on into an open field. At a command, the entire company formed into ranks by platoons and in the best training manual style pitched pup tents. We had arrived in France.

We were "on the beach" for five days. During that time we had nothing to do, and our officers made little effort to keep us occupied. We were told that it was dangerous to stray too far from our area because of mines. Several men in another company had been badly wounded when they carelessly disobeyed this order.

Most of the time we were concerned with food. Facilities at the beach were primitive. On The *Princess Astrid* we had been served 10-in-1 rations heated in the ship's galley. On the beach we had C-rations. They were heated — after a fashion. Before each meal we fell in and were marched through several fields to a place where numbers of GI wash cans had been set up. Hundreds of "heavy" C-rations had been placed in each can and the water heated. In theory this provided us with a hot meal. We passed in single file between two men, one of whom would thrust a "heavy" can into one hand. The other man handed us a "light" can.

However, by the time we got back to our own camp, the "heavy" cans were usually cold. We soon overcame this difficulty by tapping the fuel tank of a bulldozer which had been parked in our field and abandoned. The fuel oil, poured into a can of earth, made a good sooty fire. We heated, or rather reheated, our rations and made coffee over the flame. Usually by the time the food was hot enough to eat, one was as black as Al Jolson, but at least it was a warm meal.

It rained at least once almost every day and often a cold wind blew in from the sea, but only the inaction of waiting for the move we knew was coming was galling. We walked, talked and watched the company poker game which by this time had ended in a six-way split among the more expert gamblers in the company.

Finally, on the fifth night we were told to be ready to move at 3 o'clock the following morning. We packed everything except our shelter halves and were handed two days rations. The next morning, in the dark and through a light cold rain, we loaded up with our usual burden of overcoat, pack and duffle bag and trudged off on the first leg of our journey to the front.

After an hours wait in the rain, we were jammed 25 to a truck aboard vehicles. Another hours wait while we shifted about uncomfortably, and then we began to move. Because of my personal reluctance to rush into anything, I had ended up in the middle of the truck, my legs squeezed between packs, my back against the thin air and rain and my entire self in discomfort.

We drove southwest along the coast, past a prisoner-of-war camp, past seaside villages and through hedged lanes to Carentan, the railhead. We passed bomb craters and shell holes, torn up trees, knocked out tanks and other signs of war, but there was little sign of military forces about. By the time we reached Carentan, it was daylight. It had begun to rain hard. The Normandy farmers were conducting a horse fair in the village square, apparently oblivious of the battle which had lately passed them by. They ignored us as we stood dejected in the rain, waiting to board the train. A Company's usual luck failed in the loading. The train occupied in the reverse order of the alphabet; we came last, and had to stand for more than an hour as the rain dripped off our helmets, dampened our trousers and made puddles in the pockets of our GI raincoats.

When our turn came, the 45 cars were all filled. There seemed to be no room for us. For a moment, it appeared that we might be left behind, a prospect which we did not look upon with disfavor. The dilemma was solved. We were marched down the length of the train and an officer shoved us, wet, dripping and angry, one at a time, into a compartment.

I found myself in the middle of a third class compartment with eight other men and their baggage. I knew none of them and they had no desire to know me. After 15 minutes, however, I managed to find space for both myself and my baggage, and settled back into a seat, which, while it could not be termed comfortable, was at least better than standing in the rain.

A few minutes more and there was a jolt and we were off on the most fantastic train ride I have ever experienced. We were bound for a replacement depot near the town of Le Mans. It lay some 100 kilometers to the south. Our train held almost 1500 men. Half its cars were new American Transportation Corps boxcars. There were 44 men in each of these. The rest of the train was a collection of rolling stock from every railway system in Europe. The car that I was in — a French vehicle — had no windows, but did have many bullet holes. Most of the coaches were so equipped. All were stacked deep with men and equipment.

The line from Carentan to anywhere was still in a shambles because of Allied bombings. As we soon discovered, it was single-tracked all the way to Paris. Most of the rail yards along the route were smashed. Yet somehow the going and coming trains had to pass one another.

The result was a pace that was so slow it was almost a walk. We managed to make St. Lo the first afternoon. From there we were to go directly south, but when we reached some low hills, we found the way was blocked by a wreck. The train backed slowly to St. Lo, and we spent the rest of the night being shunted back and forth to allow other trains to pass.

In the morning and bright sunlight we were off again on a long circuitous route which, in the end, took us to Dreux and then all the way back through Chartes to Le Mans. By the second night we were hungry because on the first day many men had thrown their second day's rations to Frenchmen who watched along the sides of the tracks for just such behavior by Americans.

On the third evening we pulled into Dreux where a pile of boxed C and K rations had been stacked and marked by cars for our arrival. Unfortunately it was dark, there was no discipline. A horde of hungry men fell on the boxes and carried off the pile in vastly unequal shares. Other men broke into a boxcar on a nearby siding and handed out most of its stock in 10-in-1's — some of it to waiting Frenchmen — but at least no one went hungry.

Our officers (with the single exception of an old colonel from the Coast Artillery, who was supposed to deliver us to Le Mans) refused to worry and simply enjoyed themselves. Each time the train stopped — which was often — hundreds of soldiers would alight, build fires beside the tracks, begin to shave and wash, cook food and eat and simply wander around. When the train was ready to pull out, the Transportation Corps engineer would blow a long series of blasts on his whistle and food, men, hot water and other articles would go back aboard. Perhaps 15 minutes or half an hour later we would stop again and the scene would repeat itself.

Once two women got aboard, rode for a day, and then calmly got off at their destination. But most of the time the sun shone. It was warm and pleasant, and except for the problem of sleeping, not unlike a gigantic picnic.

When night came, we crouched on our third class wooden bench, hip to hip and shoulder to shoulder and tried to doze. After the second night it was much easier to get some real sleep, but the nights were a fantasia of waking and sleeping, half-remembering weird buildings in the dark, lights and sounds and a strange landscape.

On the fifth day we finally arrived at Le Mans and promptly lost 24 men who struck out for town and new adventures. The remainder of the train plunged on into some dark woods 18 miles beyond the city and ended its journey on a railroad siding.

Once there we were herded into trucks and driven through the woods to a grove of trees near a gravel road. We pitched our tents helter-skelter beneath the pines. We had arrived at the open end of the replacement pipeline.

It was one of the cruelest ways to send men to the front. We were to stay together until we reached the front line. There, just as we had begun to form friendships, we would be broken up into o groups and sent, alone and friendless into combat.

Although such a system may be efficient, it certainly is not a morale builder. A man has no loyalty to a unit, for his unit exists only to be destroyed at the front. Once on the way, he is shunted through a series of depots who often care more for themselves than for their chief commodity.

The British system of assigning men to a home base unit and then forwarding them to this unit at the front is far better, although perhaps less easy to handle.

The replacement system is a callous sort of a conveyor belt transporting an ill-disciplined mob to the front and nothing more. I hated it when I was a part of it, and even after I had been wounded and knew that I would return to my own company, I hated to go back to the front through its depots.

But whatever our feelings in those dark pine woods at Le Mans, from then on until we reached battle, we were in its grip until we got to the unit which fate, or the Army, in its divine wisdom, had chosen for us.

We remained at Le Mans for nine day and we were finally issued rifles two days after our arrival. The following day we marched to a range and fired them. Our duffle bags were taken away from us — we saw them go without much regret — and we embarked upon a regular training schedule which included a half mile dogtrot each morning before breakfast, a 12-mile march (which gave us a brief glimpse of two French villages) and lectures on everything from how to behave in France to a bazooka.

Only one incident marred the routine. A man in the fourth platoon, drunk on Calvados or some other potent French beverage, cursed out a lieutenant and was placed under arrest. The first sergeant's opinion was that he was trying evade the move to the front. If this was the case, it did him no good, for he went, nevertheless, under guard. So did we — minus the guards.

Early one afternoon A Company was loaded aboard trucks and set out all by themselves for Belgium. We rode through France all the rest of that day, toward Paris. We had, like all soldiers, been looking forward to seeing that city, but it was 10 o'clock at night when we reached its outskirts. A quick roar through blacked-out streets, a few stars shining in the Seine, some chimney pots against the sky and we were on its further side and still moving.

That night we camped farther north beside the road, and it rained. Next morning we rode through the Meuse Valley, past trees yellow in the fall, past canal locks and then into Belgium.

That country had recently been liberated. All the towns were still hung with red, yellow and black flags. Everyone waved to us as we passed. One town offered us eggs and another town offered us cider. We accepted them both. By late afternoon we arrived at Dinant and before nightfall, we were at the Third Replacement Depot.

The war was imminently closer here. At Le Mans no black-out had been enforced, but at dusk in Belgium, everything went out. The Third Depot was strung along a low ridge of hills, in a long grove of trees. The place abounded in mud, and it rained steadily after we arrived. At night we could hear RAF bombers going over into Germany. There was the usual round of lectures, but not many marches, and my chief concern was in fooling the Army out of a new green "combat" jacket. It was to stay with me to the end of the fighting.

On the fifth day after we arrived, we once again boarded trucks and drove to the depot's forward battalion in a woods outside Aachen. It was close enough to the fighting so that a battalion of 155 mm. rifles was behind it. All that night we stayed at the depot, as it sent shells whispering over our heads into the town.

During the night I had an attack of diarrhea and by morning I was sick and miserable.

5

My morale was also weakened by the break-up of the replacement company and our dispersal to various units. All the machine gunners and heavy weapons men were assigned to the First Division. The first sergeant stayed at the depot and all the officers were transferred to an officer pool. I never saw any of them again.

What remained — the riflemen — were to go to the Ninth Division. Although we did not know it at the time, we were probably lucky to have been assigned to that division.

I realize that every soldier believes his unit to be the best. But the Ninth was good. It never took on the glamour which both affected and, at times, afflicted the First or Third Divisions, yet it was "a good outfit."

The Ninth Division was a good unit for a replacement because it had enough seasoned men, even at the late stage of the war in which I entered it, to prevent it from making bloody mistakes. Its staff was good. It was conservative in many ways — for instance, training was always considered more important than recreation off the line. Yet I never felt that I was being sacrificed to foolhardiness or failures in command or planning.

The division had fought in North Africa and had been part of the retreat from Kaserine Pass. Later it had taken part in the final battle for Tunisia and had landed in Sicily. After the Sicilian campaign came to a rapid close, it, together with the First Division, was moved to England to train for the invasion of the continent. On D-plus four, it came ashore at Utah. Each, helped to take

Cherbourg and cut off the Cotentin Peninsula, fought to open the way beyond St. Lo, helped hold the line at Mortain, closed the gap at Falaise, raced through France to Mons, crossed the Meuse and went on to the German border, where it—at the time I joined the division—was fighting in the Huertgen forest below Aachen.

Division Rear headquarters was in a school house near Eupen. We rode there in trucks and arrived at noon—just in time for lunch. I was still weak from my attack of the night before, and I had eaten no breakfast at the replacement depot. The casual company, which was to look out for us until we could get to our assigned units, had only C rations, and I could not bring myself to down anything from a can.

I sat forlornly at the end of the chow line, so weak I saw spots in front of my eyes, and wished acutely that I were somewhere else. Finally, after everyone else had eaten, I managed to walk to the place where the food was being served and got a cup of coffee. This, and several pieces of bread, restored my strength and made that final day before combat easier.

For the rest of the afternoon we sat in the school yard, talking a little, very conscious of the fact that we would not see each other for a long time, if ever. Clerks began to come out of the school building with lists of men to be assigned to various units. The largest group, including almost all of the non-coms, were sent to the 60th Infantry Regiment. Several fortunate men were assigned to the division band and kept at headquarters. The rest of us went to the 39th Infantry Regiment, mostly to the 3rd Battalion.

Toward evening, trucks pulled into the school yard and we climbed aboard. As the October dusk fell, we crossed the German border near Roetgen and drove through the rolling hills into the Huertgen Forest. The countryside changed abruptly at the border. The villages we passed through — Zweifell and Roetgen — were hung with white flags and their few visible inhabitants stared sullenly at us. Here and there trees had been wrecked by shells. The roads were poorer than those in Belgium and they were covered with mud.

It was dark when we reached Service Company, camped on a bare hill, looking into a wooded valley in the Siegfried Line, as we called it. The Germans called it the Westwall. We pitched our tent in the grass, uncertain and scared. I had left all my tent pins and my tent pole at the replacement depot in a well-intentioned but misguided effort to lighten my load so my tentmate, Bill Harlan, and I were forced to use a barbed wire fence to hold up our canvas home.

Just as we were preparing to go to bed, a lone German plane flew out into the night from the direction of Aachen, two ridges to the north, and passed directly over our heads. In the valley below anti-aircraft guns began to fire sending long lazy red streaks of tracers into the sky. While we threw ourselves face down on the ground, the plane continued serenely on its way. The men from Service Company looked at us in disgust as we sheepishly got to our feet again. We had made our ignorance quite plain.

It is hard now to remember just how I felt that night, the last before I was to enter combat. I do not think that I was afraid. Instead I felt helpless in the hands of a force which was pushing me onward. There was nothing I could do to change the course of my life. I did not think of going back. Instead I began to make the adjustment which all combat soldiers must make if they are to stay

21

sane for very long. It was simply to surrender to chance, knowing that if I was to be killed, I would die, and if I was to be spared, I would live.

This conclusion is much more difficult to really take faith in, despite its obvious appearance, than it is to write it down. It meant that one had to exist from moment to moment, where before life had extended to another day, another week ,another month. It meant that this food, this sun, this hill, this blade of grass, this tree were what was important. It meant living so close to death that death became quite friendly. One no longer was afraid of dying; death often seemed the only relief from pain or fatigue. Instead the cardinal point upon which life revolved was how one was to die.

Before long, I believed that I would not live through the war. I began to measure accomplishment by little bargains I made with the imponderable force which moved me — God, or Fate or whatever it was. I would ask to live until I had reached a certain town, or until I had eaten supper that night, or until we had taken a certain landmark. I found that I rarely thought of home and seldom remembered peace. I made a great many vows which I planned to keep after the war (but few of which I ever realized) and I grasped and held, to those few concepts which I felt were permanently important.

I lived intensely and because I did I am able to remember most of what happened in that short space of my life very clearly. This is perhaps one of the reasons why the war stays with me, even now, because it was experienced with a vivid reality which peace does not have.

6

In the morning—Friday, the 13th of October 1944—we woke beneath a dirty gray sunlight, packed our equipment, ate breakfast and reloaded for our ride into the valley. The road became progressively worse as we drove into the forest. The truck floundered along through the muck, between rows of dark green firs and pines, broken by clumps of bare hardwood trees under whose barren limbs golden and red leaves lay. The evergreen trees were planted in regular rows, close together, as the woods of Germany are almost everywhere.

After we had gone several miles, we turned off the main road and halted beside a group of tents in a small clearing. These were the kitchens of the 3rd Battalion. About them stood a group of dirty, bearded men, who eyed us indifferently as we hauled our huge packs from the trucks and stood huddled together in the mud. Their only interest in us seemed to be that we had brought gas masks. This was the first time gas masks had appeared at the front for some time.

Several of them came over and examined us as if we were several sides of beef brought up for supper.

"Where in hell did you get those packs?" one of them asked me.

I began to explain that we did not think much of them either, but he ignored my explanation and went on with his critical examination of the rest of my equipment.

After 15 minutes a tall nervous man in clothes even dirtier than the cooks' came over.

"You guys for L Company?" he asked.

We told him we were.

He wore no signs of rank, but we had been told at the replacement depot that stripes and bars were seldom seen on the front, so we followed him to L Company's kitchen tent. There we were ordered to get ready to go to the front. This was something of a surprise. We thought we were already there.

Under the ungentle guiding hands of some of the kitchen crew, who made no effort to conceal their scorn, we took all our equipment, except a raincoat and a blanket and rolled it into our shelter halves. These were our "big rolls". They were to be left at the kitchen. Since we had nothing to tie these with except our tent ropes, we made a pitiful sight, trying to grasp variously our rifles, our blankets and our raincoats about us.

After we made up our big rolls, we re-assembled at the center of the kitchen tent clearing. The nervous man had disappeared. We stood and waited for him to return. He did not come back. We sat down — still the subject of some unkind words from the cooks and their helpers — and gazed dejectedly at the dark trees and the gray sky.

After an hour or so, the nervous man came grinding back into the clearing with two jeeps and two trailers.

"They need you up there right away," he said, moving his hands restlessly about his field jacket.

"Up there," did not have to be explained. We knew where it was.

"We're going to take you up to the motor pool in groups," he said. "Some of you get in those jeeps."

He counted us over and found there were 29 of us in all. Five were non-coms. He put them into the first jeep and trailer. The remainder were divided into groups of five. Five got into the trailer of the second jeep and went off down the trail after the non-coms.

After a long wait, the jeeps returned. This time I climbed aboard one of the vehicles and hanging grimly to its side, was hauled away to the motor pool. When we had gone a little way, we could see why we had come no further in the truck. The road disappeared into a muddy trail. The trailer's tires flipped mud up on the hand I held against its side. I lifted the hand to wipe it off and lurched against the man next to me. He scowled and I put it back on the trailer's side. In a moment it was muddy again.

We entered the thickest part of the forest. The trees stood 60 feet high in most places and shut the weak sun out. In the half-darkness we could see the round ends of ration cans, rusting rifles, log-covered foxholes, papers and all the traditional garbage that war leaves in its wake. Several times we passed jeeps fitted out as ambulances carrying litters on steel racks. From one ambulance a soldier, with a dazed expression and a blood-stained bandage about his head, stared vacantly at us as we passed.

We plunged down a steep hill and turned off the trail into the battalion motor pool. It was nothing more than a few vehicles parked under low trees. In its center the non-coms who had gone before us stood in a frightened group. Before long all twenty-nine of us had been re-assembled again, and we were once more in a tight little knot, waiting for further orders.

For a long time nothing happened. Noon passed,

but no one brought us any food. No one seemed interested in our welfare at all.

Then the nervous man returned. "They're having a pretty hard time up there," he said.

We nodded dumbly. Someone said, "What are they going to do with us?"

"Well, they're talking about sending you up as a platoon."

This filled us with panic. None of us had wanted to face this. We knew the front was somewhere ahead. We could hear the sound of exploding shells, and we had seen the wounded returning from the battle. But it was all so confused. Our ideas of fighting—learned from training and books—had prepared us for organization, not this chaos. To go into battle without leadership was a thought we had never considered and did not want to contemplate.

"All by ourselves?" someone said weakly.

"No. We're going to get an officer to go with you."

This made us feel better. It turned out the nervous man—his name was Sergeant Lee and he was the company supply sergeant—would be platoon sergeant, a prospect he did not seem to anticipate with pleasure.

We began to stuff clips into our rifles and to look about the woods for the enemy. None seemed apparent. Sergeant Lee disappeared again.

When he came back he told us our plans had been changed again. We were to go down to battalion forward headquarters.

We gripped our rifles tightly, gathered our raincoats and blankets and slipped and slid through the mud about a mile down a steep churned-up road to the bottom of a ravine. Here we found battalion headquarters in two German bunkers, two jeeps and a collection of worried, bearded men.

The non-coms were called out and sent to the other side of the ravine. A man whose lieutenant's bars barely showed on his shirt collar took several other men away for a roadblock. At last, the rest of us were called over to a pile of boxes. Two men handed us an extra bandolier of ammunition. Two men were given a box of hand grenades apiece. Then we were introduced to a tall thin youth with a Southern accent named Stikeleather. He told us he would take us up the other side of the ravine to the L Company Command Post.

"It's in a house over on the other side of the woods," he said. "The last fifty yards or so you'll be under enemy observation and you'll have to run across a field. Don't stop until you get to the house."

With these brief instructions he started up the road. We followed, our bandoliers bumping wildly against our chests. Before we had gone very far, the men carrying the grenade boxes stopped, broke them open and handed each of us two grenades.

So, burdened by the extra ammunition, and carrying one grenade in each hand, we climbed. Soon we were breathless and sweating, but there was no halt. We passed a German soldier, lying dead in the middle of the road, his face waxey-yellow, his eyes open and staring at the sky. Another column was stopped beside the path. We exchanged a few parting words with them as we passed. They were replacements too, on their way to G Company, just over the hill.

As we climbed, we could hear mortar shells explode

in bunches on the other side of the hill. Each time one sounded close, we all flopped in the middle of the road to the anger of Stikeleather, who knew they were too far away to do any damage.

At the top of the hill, we left the road and followed a tank track into the woods. The heavy smell of balsam filled the air and the white naked wood of broken trees gleamed in the half-darkness. In what seemed a short time, we were at the edge of the woods, facing the open field.

By now I had managed to fall back to the end of the column and was heaving along, without breath. I did not see then how I would ever be able to run across the field. But I saw the others charge forward and before I knew exactly what was happening, I had followed them.

The run was over almost before it had begun. We dashed through a little apple orchard, ran through a barnyard and staggered into the lower floor of an inn, the first building in Germeter.

A man standing at the doorway watched me as I made the last few steps and then collapsed inside, fighting to get my breath.

"Jesus Christ," he said, and turned away. I felt completely lost.

What happened at Germeter, I discovered much later, had been a near disaster. L Company had been leading the attack through the woods when it was ambushed in a ravine by Germans wearing American overcoats and helmets. The first and second platoons—which had been leading the company—had been cut off and almost of all of the men in them had either been killed or captured. Only Sergeant Percer, the second platoon sergeant and the first platoon leader and one other man had escaped.

L Company's line had been bent back in a bow and for a time it appeared that the Germans might break through and sweep across the battalion. Until now it had held. When we arrived only the third and fourth platoons remained, and they were understrength from several days of hard fighting. It was a bad day, one of the worst the company ever experienced.

But we knew little of this as we arrived in the company CP. We sprawled in the straw of a manger in the basement of the inn, afraid to move for fear we would be in the way, while runners came and went and everyone ignored us.

It was a theatrical betting. Everyone was bearded and dirty and tired. I felt as if I were at a movie, but with the unpleasant knowledge that I was unable to get up and walk out of the theater. Our shelter in the inn was much like the dugouts of World War I. It was long and narrow with a low concrete roof. At the far end was a doorway which led to a larger room. Just off the doorway was another, smaller room where the actual CF group had gathered. Beyond it, in the large room, a heavy machine gun had been set upon a table and faced out three windows, none of which had glass in them.

Another gun had been set up upstairs, I found out later, although I never got to see it. The inn was, in fact, a blockhouse, with walls four feet thick, and when now and then a German shell crashed into its upper floors, no one, except we replacements, bothered to duck.

Chickens still scratched in the manger, having been spared by some miracle from the stew pot. Outside in the yard lay a row of disinterred Teller mines and just beyond them was a hedge which shut off any further view. It was not possible to show a light at night, however, and that was why the CP group had moved into the closet-like confines of the little room by the doorway.

As we were getting our breath back, the door to this inner sanctum opened and Sergeant Madeley, the company first sergeant, came out. His face was covered with a five days' beard, his hair was long and tousled and his clothes were filthy. He glared at us lying in the straw of the manger and rasped in the hoarsest voice I had ever heard, "Men, this is a fighting outfit."

No one, in view of our journey to get this far, sought to dispute this statement.

"Any of you machine gunners?" he asked.

No one was.

I ventured to say that I could speak German, an accomplishment Sergeant Lee had told me might be needed up front.

"We got plenty of guys who can do that," Madeley said, and I shut up.

That was the substance of our welcome to Company L, and I never had any reason to believe that it was anything except "a fighting outfit."

By the time the first sergeant had finished, it had begun to get dark. We were shown a C ration box, told to help ourselves, and then informed we would have to stand guard on the four corners of the building during the night. One non-com, Sergeant Jones, had come up the hill with us. He was assigned to arrange the reliefs.

Since we had not a watch between us, we had to use our own estimates of the time. Each of us was to stand an hour's guard outside the door to the yard. Night came, a night full of half-sleep, long periods of straining and straining to pierce the darkness, of exploding shells in the distance and the rush of a cold wind through the narrow chamber. I only half remember parts of what happened.

I remember a wounded man from G Company who stumbled in from the woods with a piece of grenade lodged in his leg.

"I threw it at him," he kept saying, "and he was so close, I got hit with my own grenade."

I remember Stikeleather coming back from the woods after repairing a break in the wire and telling someone how a broken tree had almost fallen on him.

I remember a wounded man from the 2nd Battalion, who had been struck in the penis by shrapnel from our own artillery. I asked him how it felt, and he said, "It hurts like hell."

I remember getting a Browning Automatic Rifle stuck in my ribs when I relieved one of the men on guard. He was very frightened and had stood guard only 20 minutes (by my estimate) before he asked for relief.

I stood two shifts that night, and when morning came I was glad. I had lain through the long hours near the center of the narrow room and shivered instead of sleeping.

Morning did arrive finally, and surprisingly, the sun shone. The machinegunners cooked breakfast, ignoring us, just as they did the chickens. The day wore on, while we sat huddled against the concrete wall, a part of nothing. We did not even speak to each other.

Just after noon, Madeley came out of his cubbyhole and told Sergeant Jones to take five of us down to fill a gap in the line between L and K Companies. I was one of the five selected.

Fearfully, we loaded up our gear and followed Stikeleather back across the field into the woods. This, as we had often heard, was it. We were going into combat.

We could hear the steady crash of mortar shells falling in clusters below us in the woods as we went. We dodged and wove through the felled pines and broken boughs until we came to the third platoon CP. The air was heavy with the sickly sweet smell of the trees, and the woods were oppressively close and forbidding. At the CP, Stikeleather introduced us to Lieutenant Toujay, the only officer left in the company. He was short and thin and he had dark skin. He seemed very tired, but he smiled at us.

"We've got a little gap to fill," he said, sadly, as if he regretted this imposition on our lives.

We said nothing.

"The Jerries are dropping mortars on the hill so you may get a little fire. They're sore because they didn't break through yesterday."

He called his platoon sergeant over and we followed him silently down the steep slope into the draw, ducking now and then at the sound of the shells. Near the bottom, we stopped and were parceled out, two to a foxhole.

Beyond us we saw blank row after row of trees, set close together. To our right we could barely make out another hole, hidden in broken boughs. We could not see the hole on our left at all. Jones and I crouched down in the little hollow in the earth and Jones immediately began to make it deeper.

In a little while a tall man with fierce eyes and a face like a wolf came from the left, the L Company side. He told us he was Sergeant Kosik, our squad leader. He walked about unconcerned and apparently completely unafraid, yet with a slight crouch, as if he expected something to suddenly pass just over his shoulders.

"See them," he said, and pointed out into the trees. We looked and noticed for the first time two dark green coats and beneath them the bodies of two dead Germans. "They tried to infiltrate last night, I shot them."

He said it just as he would have said, "I was thirsty so I got a drink of water."

"There's nothing to worry about," he added. "We've got a booby trap out there so we'll know if they're coming."

Then he went away, and Jones began to dig again.

Another man came past wearing a mud-soaked overcoat. He looked at Jones, frantically spading up light brown earth, and said sadly, "That won't do no good."

Then he walked away down the line and we never saw him again.

The platoon sergeant from G Company came over and talked to us for a while.

"If you see anything out there that locks like GI's, don't shoot," he said. "K Company's going to attack and straighten the line."

All the time the mortars kept traversing the hill. Each time we heard them whistle, we ducked and

Jones looked fearfully at me. Because he was afraid and showed it, I was determined that I would not be, and I used my scorn of his fear to drive some of my own terror away.

Suddenly a concentration of mortar shells crashed about our hole. Jones scrambled down as far as he could into the little square pit and pressed against me. I felt my helmet rise from my head with the explosion and then settle back over my eyes. Neither of us were hurt, but off to the right, I heard someone cry, "Medic! Medic!"

I was filled with a great desire to leave. I had never wanted to leave anywhere as badly as I wanted to get out of that hole. Jones, thoroughly scared now, had stopped his digging and was crouched down at my knees, silent with fright.

We heard the crackling sound of rifles begin as K Company tried to move forward through the woods. I put my own rifle on the edge of the hole and looked out, but I could see nothing except the two dead Germans and the dark regular rows of pine trees. Bullets went overhead with a familiar crack-pop sound that meant they were close, and I hunched my head down between my shoulders and tried to compromise my fear with the duty I felt to watch for the enemy.

The attack stopped after about five minutes and mortar shells began to fall again, but they were farther away down the line this time. In a few minutes our friend from G Company came back down the line and stopped by our hole again.

"Couple of your buddies got hit," he said, in a conversational way.

"Who?" I asked. I hardly knew the men's names.

"Oh, big tall blond fellow and his buddy. Got cut up around the face."

"Very bad?"

"I don't know. Lot of blood," the sergeant said.

We said nothing. It was difficult for us to understand. They had been on the front line only 15 minutes, and they had been wounded.

"Some of us are lucky and some of us aren't," the sergeant said.

"What happened to the attack?" I asked. It seemed perfectly logical that it should have achieved its purpose.

"I don't know," the sergeant said. "I guess something went wrong."

This seemed incredible to me. I had yet to discover that plans in war rarely go as they are supposed to. If an attack had been planned, it seemed to me that it should have accomplished its purpose, and I viewed with little comprehension an effort that got nowhere. The world seemed to have lost its balance for a time. I suppose now I wanted that attack to succeed so we could be free to get out of our hole and go back where we had come from. Its failure to release me from the woods stands out as one of the biggest disappointments of the war.

We were in the woods for three more hours before Kosik came to tell us the company had been "pinched out" by the 1st battalion. This was just as puzzling as the failure of K Company to get us loose from our predicament for we had heard no firing nor had we seen anyone in front of us. Yet now the entire platoon rose from its holes and balked calmly back through the woods up the hill toward the road.

We assembled near the two pillboxes which marked battalion headquarters and there found the rest of the company and the remainder of the 29 replacements. Among them were the men who had been taken off the day before to guard the roadblock. One of them asked me where we had been.

"On the line," I said, proudly. I had come through my baptism of fire.

7

That evening we climbed back out of the ravine and camped in a dense grove of trees where it was so dark that no one could see his hand, even if he held it directly in front of his face. During the night 80 more replacements came to the company and the next day 30 more arrived, bringing it back to something near regular strength.

We rested three days while we were reorganized into a military establishment. All the veterans of the third platoon—some of whom had seen less than a week of action—were made squad leaders. The replacements were counted off into squads. Those who were left over where made machine gunners or mortar men, though they knew little or nothing about these weapons.

Jones, because he had been a sergeant in training, was made my squad leader. His assistant was John Munk, a former policeman from Albany, New York.

Jones was of middle height with a narrow, not very pleasant face. He had a sharp chin, a pointed nose which just missed being hooked, and an unhappy disposition. He was from Ohio, but he spoke with a twang which I associated with Kentucky, and I believe he lived near the border between the two states.

His constant nervous fear, combined with my experience with him on the front, made me dislike him. He was not a leader, and he knew it, but unfortunately, he tried to make us believe that he knew what he was doing. Perhaps I am too harsh with him now in memory, but most of my recollection of him is unpleasant.

I also disliked Munk, but for another reason. He had

come to the division only a few weeks before and had been in combat for only a few days before being slightly wounded. After a short stay at an evacuation hospital he had returned to the front.

Because he had been under fire and because he had been wounded, he was made an assistant squad leader. But he was slow in both movement and thought, and he complained a great deal about minor annoyances.

His greatest disability was the peculiar and pessimistic way in which he could talk. Until we got used to it, we would listen to him and when he was through, be convinced that the war was almost over, we were losing and we would spend the rest of our lives in a prisoner of war camp.

Luckily, his aversion to fighting quickly eliminated him from his job.

The second group of replacements, who arrived after we returned from the front, included one who became the Browning Automatic Rifleman in our squad. His name as Donald Marshall, and he was to be my best friend through most of the war.

Marshall was only 20 years old, a tall gangly boy who had the ability to seem to shamble when he walked, yet who moved with considerable grace and speed over the ground. The product of Chemical Warfare Service basic training, a stay at Boston University as an ASTP student and, like myself, some time in the 78th Division, he was eventually to become a second lieutenant.

Although he was a year younger than I, I found myself respecting his judgment. I could talk to him too, as I could to no one else in the squad, for we felt the same way about the war. It was still a great adventure.

Looking back on it now, I know we were foolish. We had seen almost no fighting, and we were eager to get to the front. Battle as still exciting and the excitement hid war's true value. To us, it was still part of a big game, one which had new rules to be learned and for which there were special tools and understanding to be mastered.

With the attack at Germeter, the 39ᵗʰ Infantry's part of the fighting in the Forest came temporarily to a standstill. It had begun to rain and the dirt roads of the area were little rivers of mud, churned into a liquid cocoa brown by jeeps and the feet of marching men. The yellow/red leaves of the hardwood trees grew soggy and gray. The pines dripped monotonously night and day. Their heavy boughs shut out any sun, making it impossible for clothes to dry.

It was a miserable time in my life. The woods inflicted a great dampness of soul too, because of their forbidding darkness and their confining blank sameness. The days were short, and when night came, it was impossible to see or do anything. We ran lengths of telephone wire out to our outposts so we could find our way about in the darkness. Once I remember we did not do this. Munk and I spent most of our relief trying to find our way back into our tents so we could wake the next watch.

I also remember the night we moved from the bivouac area, where we had been in reserve, back to Germeter. We were to leave before dawn so that we could be through the town and into our positions on its far side by daybreak. All of our equipment, except our blankets, had been packed and assembled the night before. We were awakened at 4 a.m. It was as dark as if we'd been struck totally blind. Attempts to assemble platoons and squads were unsuccessful.

Finally, on a shouted order from the company commander, everyone faced the sound of his voice, then we faced right and crashed wildly through the trees toward the road. Here there was at least a lighter darkness of sky stretching like a thin ribbon over our heads, above the high black walls of the trees.

We began to march, slipping and sliding in the mud. It was still so dark that one simply could not see the man ahead. The only way to keep in file was to guide on the sky and the slop, slop of feet in the mud. When the feet ahead stopped, it was time to stop. There were endless collisions in the darkness, curses and confusion, and although it was only a few miles from our reserve area to Germeter, it took us almost until dawn to reach the town.

Then, as we came out on higher ground, the Germans began to send up flares. These helped guide us to our positions. Still, there was a constant inter-mingling of units and it was unbelievable that when day finally did arrive, we were all in our holes. The relief had been accomplished.

Marshall, Munk and I occupied what had been an air raid shelter. Before the day was over, it also was the home of the reserve squad of the platoon, a situation which hardly made for comfort. The shelter was built in the form of a shallow tunnel, covered with boards and dirt. At one end stood a ladder. A bomb had blown a hole in the dirt wall at the other end. A wooden bench stood against one wall, and the tunnel was so narrow that only one man at a time could move through it. Because of enemy observation and shell fire, we could not get out of the place during the daylight.

Altogether, it would have been an impossible

situation had an attack developed. Fortunately none did, and we spent each day sitting dully on the bench, listening to shells explode above us.

Because we were unable to get out of the shelter during the day, we were forced to submit to certain indignities in attending to bodily elimination. Usually we saved the by-products from this daily chore until it got dark. Then we would either carry them up the ladder and outside, or if we were less brave, simply toss them as far from the tunnel entrance as we could.

I remember one night I was sitting at the end of the bench near the ladder when one of the men from the reserve squad tossed out a can full of his urine. Unfortunately, he threw it in the wrong direction. I was saved from a bath only because it was nearly bedtime, and I was wearing my raincoat.

That same night as I lay on the tunnel floor trying to sleep, I had the added indignity of being stepped on. A man had mistaken me for the dirt floor. By that time, I had begun to feel like dirt.

We were to stay at the front for five days, but on the morning of the fourth day, we were relieved by the 28th Division, which was to see bitter action in the Forest. The Ninth, badly understrength and tired from the long drive across France and Belgium, was ordered into First Army reserve. It left 3,836 men behind as casualties in the Forest. Only the Fourth Division suffered more there.

8

After we were relieved, we walked back toward the Belgian border under a rainy sky. We were loaded onto trucks for our move to a reserve area. It was cold and unmistakably winter, and we hoped we were being sent to a town or a village instead of another woods. We left the Forest in the afternoon, crossed the Belgian border and drove south through the gloomy early twilight. We joked feebly about living in houses, but we did not really believe that we would.

After dark, and after we had gone perhaps 40 miles, we turned off a concrete highway into a low plot of newly planted trees. Then in low gear, we moved, stopped, moved and stopped, until at last, we halted in another forest of pines. Just as our journey ended, a 105 mm. rifle fired nearby, sending a shell over our heads. We were still not very far from the front.

Marshall and I were so disgusted that we did nothing toward making a camp that night. We put on our raincoats, threw our blankets over us and laying our heads on our big rolls, went to sleep.

The next morning we were more cheerful. We found we were camped in a patch of forest between the towns of Elsenborn and Kalterherberg, on the edge of the Ardennes. The front line, lightly held, lay four or five miles beyond our area over the high wooded hills.

It was a quiet sector and we never saw anyone else. We were there for almost three weeks before we moved again, the longest time we ever spent in any one place during the rest of the war. Before the morning was over, and for obvious reasons, we christened it Mud Valley.

Considerable change took place in the company during our stay. Officers were shifted about, squads re-organized, equipment cleaned and new equipment added. Shortly after our arrival, we were assigned Lieutenant (later Captain) McClellan as company commander. He was a tall man with a pleasant face which always seemed to be smiling. His voice was thin and rather high, but it was also clear and gentle. I never saw him angry, and he seldom shouted, except at a formation. He had been with I Company in North Africa and Sicily and had been badly wounded in Normandy. After briefly returning to the United States to convalesce, he had come back to the front. Under his command we began to become an infantry unit, instead of being a partly organized mob.

But if we were now fortunate in having a fine company commander, we were less lucky with platoon leaders. After several other officers in the Forest, Lieutenant Belt took over the second platoon. A short, dapper man with a tiny moustache, Belt was unpopular before a week had passed. Today I cannot explain exactly why. Chiefly, I suppose, it was because he did not inspire confidence in his ability. He did not have that magic quality of leadership which is impossible to adequately define, but which, when present, is so vital in an infantry officer.

Then, too, he was a part of the general dissatisfaction we felt toward Jones and Sergeant Percer, the platoon sergeant, at least to Marshall and me.

Percer, so thin and cadaverous that he sometimes seemed almost dead, had been fighting for a long time. He was from the Carolinas and had a hot Southern temper. He had been in North Africa, Sicily and almost everything beyond and his sharp temper had been worn down to a fine edge by such a long grind. He was one of the few men to escape from the ambush at Germeter, and he had seen many replacements come and go that we were of little importance to him at the time.

Yet he was a good platoon sergeant, one of the best I ever knew. He moved with a well disciplined instinct, carrying an M-l rifle with him where ever he went, as if it were a part of him, his thin pointed chin, his hot angry eyes and his sallow skin, as white as a skull beneath his helmet. But he — and the rest of the veterans of North Africa and Sicily — did not accept us for a long time.

Being a combat infantryman is like joining a lodge, certain degrees must be passed before one can become a full member of the order. If you have been at a certain place, helped take a certain town, undergone a certain barrage, you are accepted. If you have not done these things and have not shared the common experience of being very close to death, you must sit humbly on the edge of the circle and await your opportunity to enter.

Some men never make it. They are killed or wounded before they come to know this feeling. Some are partially initiated, but do not ever completely belong. It is a strange comradeship and one which it is very difficult to explain to anyone who has not been under fire. It persists often after the war, and I have felt its effect in conversations with friends, even in civilian life.

Because we had done nothing but arrive at the front, sit on it, and then retire, we were outsiders through our stay at Mud Valley. We were the ones to whom the cooks gave the least food. We got the worst PX rations and the dirtier details, and most of the time we sat and griped about it.

Each morning we had training. We marched to clearings in the woods by companies and were lectured or forced to perform various combat problems.

In the afternoons we sat around fires in our company areas and wrote letters, talked, and complained. Food, as usual, was our principal worry. We were always hungry, and there did not ever seem to be enough to eat.

At night there was nothing to do but crawl into our tents and sleep. Sometimes it rained, but we were used to it by this time, and we paid it little attention.

Privately Marshall and I were agreed that Jones, the squad leader, was useless; Lieutenant Belt was a poor officer and Percer was unreasonable. There seemed little we could do about the situation.

Then just before we were ordered back to the front again, a chance for something new appeared. Until that time, each company had had its own reconnaissance patrol, a group of volunteers attached to the company headquarters group. This unit did most of the patrolling for the company, except for combat patrols, since these usually required more than the five men it contained. A few days before we moved from Mud Valley to relieve the 4th Division, a call for volunteers for a battalion patrol to replace this system was made.

Battalion patrol members were given special privileges, clothes and equipment with the understanding that their work would be more dangerous than regular frontline rifle platoon duty.

9

Marshall and I talked over the offer, but we were still undecided when we moved to the new positions south of Butgenbach in the high rolling hills of the Hohe Venn.

We rode most of the way to the front in trucks. It was a lonely country with only the woods, a few farm fields and one or two towns. It was somber, too, in the late fall with the black-green of the pines, the gray untilled fields, the empty farm houses and silent villages. We detrucked near the edge of a large patch of forest and marched several miles into its interior to the front.

The company CP was located in a log hut, built by the 4th Division. Beyond it along the far edge of the woods stretched the front line on approximately the same points as the German-Belgian border. The platoon was spread thinly below the crest of a long ridge, in the trees. Square points of woods jutted out toward the top of the ridge in several places, but we could scarcely cover them, for our company alone had relieved an entire battalion of the 4th.

Instead, we set up a series of outposts along the main line of resistance and connected them with sound power telephones on a circuit which ran to the platoon CP. The platoon CP, in turn, was part of a company wire net.

The first squad—seven men strong—was divided into two parts. Marshall, Munk, Jones, Duck and the platoon sniper and bazooka man took over a point of woods at the right end of the platoon line. The rest of the squad was to our left and rear about 150 yards away with the crew of a light machine gun.

From our woods near the top of the hill we could look across a valley to two German bunkers barely visible in another row of trees. Off to the right several miles away was a German village. Directly in front of us on the crest of the ridge was a paved road which ran parallel with the front. Trees, which had once lined both its sides, had been chopped down by the Germans and lay across the pavement to prevent traffic.

Over the crest of the hill stretched the endless row of concrete tank barriers known as "dragon's teeth."

The 4th Division had dug foxholes in the woods and roofed them over with pine logs so that we were fairly comfortable. Boredom was the only real foe we had. There was nothing to do but sit. We lived for meal times. Breakfast and supper were served hot at the company CP's hut. Each morning and evening we trudged down the hill, picked up our chow, and trudged back to the front line to eat it. In theory, one third of the men at any one outpost were supposed to eat at a time, but usually there was almost no one at the outposts during meal hours. The impatient and hungry men left behind at the top of the hill refused to wait until the first party had returned. We got so careless that we did not even take our weapons with us.

During the daylight hours, we visited a great deal, walking the length of the platoon line from end to end. It was a good way to keep warm.

It snowed the fourth day after we arrived — the first snow of the winter — and by next morning two feet of damp white covered the ground. Another day and there was a brief thaw. The snow dropped from the trees into the woods with great plumps of sound and soaked through our clothes. I had brought my overcoat with me and by the end of the day it was wet through. Later I wrapped it in my big roll and I do not believe it dried out until spring came.

Each night was an eternity of standing guard. Because there were so few men at each outpost and because the nights were now a part of winter, reliefs grew longer and longer. At our outpost, we stood a three hour and 45 minute shift, went to bed until nearly morning, and then were wakened to stand another hour.

Jones refused to stand any guard at all—claiming a States-side privilege which removed non-coms from such duty—and we hated him for it. He spent most of each day and all night crouched in his hole with the telephone. When he did emerge, it would be with chattering teeth and a large red nose which dripped in the cold. Munk stayed with him in the hole, coming to the surface less often than his leader.

Despite all these inconveniences, Marshall and I enjoyed ourselves. The 4th Division had laid booby traps made of hand grenades in the grass beyond the edge of the woods and had rigged cans loaded with pebbles on wires among the trees. We extended this line of devices by loosening the pins on fragmentation grenades and attaching their rings to short pieces of scrap telephone wire. The result probably would have fooled no German patrol, but we felt secure behind our ring of fortifications.

One such trap, however, almost led me to disaster. I had been following the line of grenades along the edge of the woods until I came to what I thought was the last one. I lifted my foot to step out into the field for a closer look, and then some instinct made me stop and look down. My instep was poised over a tightly stretched piece of telephone wire which ran to a grenade lashed to the base of a nearby tree. I carefully lowered my foot to the ground, sweated for a moment and then went back the way I had come.

Only two incidents marred the near peace of our stay in the woods. The first took place the night the snow fell.

Marshall and I had been on guard listening to the conversation on the telephone. Percer broke in and whistled for his hourly check of posts up and down the line. Everyone checked in except the far left flank outpost, the one nearest the pillboxes on the hill.

After some discussion about this and no further word from the outpost leader, Hugel, squad leader of the third squad, said, "I'm agoin' up and have a look."

Fifteen minutes later Percer checked again. Someone at Hugel's phone said, "He ain't back yet."

A half hour passed with two more calls from Percer and Hugel had still not returned. Marshall and I stared off into the falling snow, seeing the round little man running down the wire in the darkness with his fingers, tracing it over rocks and around tree trunks. We wondered—as everyone must have silently—if the Germans had cut it and were waiting for him in ambush.

Finally, just as we were to wake our relief and go to bed, Hugel's Ohio drawl come back on the line. "A tree fell over and broke her," he said. "We got her fixed now."

Then we heard the voice of the squad leader at the far outpost, and we went to bed peacefully relieved.

The second incident was as amusing, although it could have been more serious. We had just begun to get sleeping bags, a new and more comfortable way to sleep than blankets. They were issued on a seniority basis, the first going to the men who had been at the front the longest. The night mine arrived, I went off to a hole by myself, took off my shoes (a luxury I could not afford) and bedded down for the night.

I had just finished struggling into the bag and had pulled its zipper up to my chin, when I heard shots. I crawled out again, my heart pounding more rapidly than usual and ran to the edge of the woods and jumped down into a standing foxhole we had dug for such emergencies.

"Somebody let a burp gun go off over Hugel's head," Marshall said.

We looked out into the darkness, straining our eyes for the sight of a human form. Shots sounded to our left at Hugel's outpost, and mortar shells and flares began to explode in front of us. The flares revealed nothing except the bare shape of the hill covered with snow.

I took out a piece of chewing gum I had saved from my K ration that day and munched away. Hugel's outpost began to shoot rifle flares and rifle grenades, but they would not explode in the soft snow. A steady volume of fire—all American—kept up on our left. The right flank, the third platoon, was silent.

Suddenly Marshall hissed for me to be quiet and said, "What was that?"

I stopped chewing my gum.

"What?" I said.

"I don't hear it now... There, that."

It was my gum. I had been popping it loudly, a habit I have.

"Next time chew a little softer," Marshall said, sourly.

I closed my mouth, but I kept on chewing and searching the dark hill. Something caught my eye, a darker shape against the snow. I looked at it again. It seemed to move. We had been told to not fire unless necessary for we did not want the Germans to know how lightly our line was held. I fired.

"What was that?" Marshall whispered.

"I thought I saw something," I said, calmly.

Back in his hole, Munk was on the telephone.

"Send us more men, we're being counter-attacked," he shouted.

Percer angrily told him to shut up and ordered a mortar flare. When it exploded, I saw that my German had turned into a bush. The alarm subsided while I went into a temporary disgrace. The blame eventually fell on Munk, however, for becoming almost hysterical.

With that, our stay at the front came to an end. We were relieved by the 99th Division, its first visit to the front. They were a day late in arriving and they took a long time to get to their positions after they finally got to the company CP.

We marched back to our trucks, loaded them in a fine cold drizzle and late in the afternoon of the same day went back to Mud Valley, our former bivouac area.

10

During our stay at the front, Marshall and I made up our minds. We went to battalion headquarters the next day and asked about the patrol.

Plans for its formation, we found, were still not detailed: The idea originated with Lieutenant Saddle, the battalion intelligence officer. What he wanted was a squad of six men from each of the three rifle companies. He promised us combat suits, all the automatic weapons we could get, no guard duty or KP, no work details and special training.

I told him I could speak German, but he was not eager to admit me to the patrol because I wore glasses. Since this handicap had neither prevented me from getting into the infantry or a rifle platoon, I could not see why it should keep me out of the patrol, and after some argument I finally got his reluctant approval. But all during my stay, I had difficulty in getting into action. Saddle may have been correct in fearing that my glasses might give a patrol away, but I still think I was right.

He was an odd sort of an officer anyway. In civil life he had been a rifle and pistol salesman, and he was a crack shot, yet he wore glasses and had miserable eyesight for an infantry officer. He was 37, tall and thin with a tan light, and almost hairless face which made him seem much younger. He talked in a meticulous way with great deliberateness and a precise, sometimes unpleasant, quality.

His worst faults were his great clumsiness (he could fall into any hole) and a Boy Scout attitude toward the war which was half the sort of stuff one reads in boys' adventure magazines and half a deep and abiding faith in the field manual as a Bible. These two things often made him seem absurd, although he tried very hard to be a good officer. He was very loyal to the patrol and defended us to the last, once telling the headquarters company commander — who saw us for what we were — that we had more courage in our little fingers "than any man in your company."

The other members of the patrol were a strange collection of good, bad, and indifferent. From L Company, besides Marshall and myself, came Hugel, the roly-poly squad leader; Pelky, a member of Hugel's squad; Ellis, his buddy, and Spooner, a friend of Hugel's who had been wounded and who had just returned to combat.

From I Company we got Pappy, a Regular Army veteran of laying mines on the beaches of Hawaii, who had never seen combat; Lavender, a boy about Marshall's age; Riesinger, a harsh-voiced tall man from the Midwest, and a quiet fellow of indeterminate age with a moustache named Harris,

K Company sent Kiser, a pimply-faced youth; Thorpe, his buddy; Wright, a big farmer, and Presiado, Villegas, and Perez, three Mexican-Americans from California. Perez was non-descript, Presiado was only 18 or 19 and often silly, and Villegas was a silent, but deadly man, who loved his M-l rifle like a wife, and who had ears and eyes like a cat.

As soon as he could get us all together, Lieutenant Saddle took me with him to regimental supply and we begged what we could in equipment. We were unable to get combat suits so we settled instead for mackinaws. Each man received a carbine for his personal use, fitted with a grenade launcher of dubious value, and, in addition, we created a weapons pool in which we placed two "grease guns", two Thompson submachine guns, a couple of M-1 rifles, grenades, rifle grenades, booby trap igniters of various kinds, several pounds of TNT in quarter pound blocks and two pounds of tetral with prima cord and a box of blasting caps and some fuse.

We also were able to get a pyramidal tent. We set it up several hundred yards away from the rest of the battalion and there we lounged to the anger and envy of the men from the various rifle companies.

Technically, we were still assigned to the rifle companies and only attached to battalion headquarters. Our pay and rank still came from them. Because we did no work or performed no guard duty, we were soon outcasts from our own companies. Now I can see why they were angry, although I could not then. All companies were understrength and most of the time we appeared to be wasting our time, which, in fact, we were.

Our special training consisted of firing heavy and light machine guns in the valley of the Roer behind our camp (one day), and of demonstrating how to lay booby traps. This latter was Lieutenant Saddle's idea. He knew more about it than anyone else in the battalion, but even he was not too proficient. During one demonstration he blew up the igniter and slightly wounded himself in the face.

When we had nothing else to do, we went on "patrols." We hunted deer in the woods across the valley, poked about looking for firewood, and several times we walked across the hills to Kalterherberg. I remember these latter trips very clearly.

Kalterherberg was strung along a ridge to the north of the woods in which we were bivouacked, a long line of timbered houses, all of them abandoned by the Germans before we arrived in the valley. A part of the village stretched down the ridge to the river and ran up the further slope. The Roer was the border boundary, and the, houses across the river had been left untouched, but the major part of the village had been ruthlessly looted.

Bedding had been ripped from beds, papers torn from drawers, dishes broken end scattered about, pictures removed from walls and windows smashed. Trails of mud from many feet ran from house to house, and in most houses the debris led into the yard and lay beneath the windows where it had been thrown by thoughtless hands.

Barn doors had been ripped off and carted away to make huts in the woods, while the cattle of the town wandered up and down its single street with no one to milk or care for them. It was a pitiful sight, one which haunted me almost as much as any other that remains from the war. It was the first looted town I ever saw, and I did not like it. I don't know who began the destruction; I don't think it was the 9th Division, although it doesn't matter much.

It was the beginning of looting which carried all the way across Germany and for which there was no excuse or any justification, save that the Germans had done the same thing in other countries. Still I am not proud to have been a part of it.

We went to the town several times. Once we brought back—for no useful purpose—a horse and a carriage. We kept the horse hidden in the woods near our camp for awhile, but he eventually wandered away. Once we drove home a cow and slaughtered her in the woods at night to provide fresh beef for the battalion kitchen.

We also stole from our own division. During the night — using the excuse that we were practicing for patrols — we swiped boxes of K rations from company kitchens. We took a stove from the 2nd Battalion. The only thing we were unable to procure was a lamp. This lack of light would bother us all the time the patrol was together. We never completely solved the problem. Most of the time we burned gasoline in a can, but it was an unhealthy, dangerous illumination. For a while we used bacon grease. It was a satisfactory, although pungent, light.

When our lamp went out or it became to dangerous to keep burning, there was nothing to do but go to bed. Even so, we were better off than most of the men in the rifle companies, who had no lights at all.

For a short while I got away from the rest of the patrol by going to regimental interrogation school. My German was ungrammatical, and what little I had picked up in college and high school was hardly enough to keep up with the German-born members of the interrogation team, but each morning I'd ride down to Elsenborn, sit in a warm house with them, drink coffee and listen to them talk.

I did learn a little, especially military terms, which were valuable to me later. But I am afraid I was of no help to the patrol.

Thus we "Rangers", as the rest of the battalion called us, spent the remainder of our rest in the woods. We sat in front of our tent around a fire and watched the rest of the battalion hand-carry supplies into the muddy area, or saw them build a corduroy road of logs to the highway. We smoked and talked, ate from our secret supply of K rations, and Marshall and I even went to the 5th Corps rest camp at Eupen for two days.

On December 4th, the regiment finally moved north again into the Rhineland. The rifle companies went first. We trailed behind with the kitchens. Early in the morning we heard the men from the rifle companies passing our tent. They cursed as they slipped and fell in the mud where the corduroy road ended, bumping against one another, and then moving on to the hard road at the edge of the woods where they were to load trucks.

Long after they had gone, we struck our tent and followed. It took us all that day to catch the rest of the battalion. We were bound for the town of Schevenhuette near the edge of the Huertgen Forest. We drove north, parallel to the front, through Malmedy and Spa. The trees along the roads were stripped bare. The land was gray everywhere: gray tree trunks, gray stone buildings, gray sky, gray dead leaves and the fallow gray of the fields. Even the clothes of the towns people seemed gray and a gray prevailing gloom hung in the air.

East of Eupen were only the wrecks of towns, ripped up and down by shells, their bare rafters showing to the sky, the walls splintered and holed, the interiors heaved out into the street like vomit, dirty and nauseous. Dead cows lay unburied in the fields beside the dirty white ribbons of engineers' tape spread to mark pathways through minefields.

We turned north again toward Aachen and passed through the Siegfried Line. Like a paradox, it was white and untouched in places, its concrete bunkers clean and immaculate. Aachen, itself, was burned, blasted and empty. At its edge a new school house, built within the past few years, was as bleak and as bare as a monument with all its windows gone and its interior blackened by fire. Heaps of broken bricks and roof tiles lay in the streets, making it difficult for vehicles to pass. The large newly-built modern houses on the edge of the city were hurt, too, and somehow they seemed less able to take the damage than the older buildings in the center of the city which stood with an ancient sort of grace against the winter wind.

It was an bitter, ugly landscape, one we were seeing for the first time. Always before this, we had caught only glimpses: in France, the railroad yards; in Belgium, a house or two; in the Forest, smashed trees. But here the entire view of human existence had suffered a change. It was as if a giant steamroller had moved across the land, sparing nothing as it went.

When we arrived in Schevenhuette, the battalion rear CP, it was almost night. The rest of headquarters and the rifle companies had moved up into the hills and woods beyond the town, to relieve the 1st Division. The 1st had been hit hard. One of its regiments had tried to capture the village of Merode on the Rhine plain beyond the woods. The attack had been made by two companies, and all had gone well until they suddenly discovered there was no one on their flanks.

Then German tanks cut in behind them and isolated and slaughtered them. The woods were full of dead. In one small area we counted 25 dead Germans. American dead had already been picked up and buried when we arrived, but no one had had time to bury the Germans. They lay where they had fallen among the pitiful leftovers of the battlefield.

Because we were the last to arrive, and because Lieutenant Saddle was too busy to look out for us, we were billeted in a stable. Its foul smell was increased because someone also had used it for a latrine. But we were enterprising and before long Riesinger found us a place to sleep on the top floor of a nearby house. The room had only bare boards of the floor, but they were clean and dry.

The downstairs belonged to the crew of an 8-inch gun emplaced across the road behind a shattered sawmill. The roof of the house had been partially blown away and all its timbers were weak. All night long it swayed as the gun fired across the hills to the plain beyond. I remember waking and sleeping with the blasts and wondering, in a detached sort of way, if the house might collapse before morning, with all of us in it.

By the next morning Lieutenant Saddle had finished his other duties and had time to come around and see us. He told us to divide the patrol into thirds. Two-thirds were to go up to the battalion forward CP., while the rest would remain behind with the equipment in Schevenhuette.

We took what we thought we would need and set off up the muddy set of wheel tracks into the woods above town. It was a slow climb past a small stone castle to the CP, a clearing where two trails came together. The trees here were not so high or close together as they had been near Germeter, but they were still the same somber dark green or black. No snow lay on the ground, but there had been enough rain to make it difficult for even jeeps to get through.

The actual forward command post was in a dugout roofed over with boards. Its walls were made of sandbags and beside its door stood a white sign which read "Nudge Blue Battle CP". Nudge was the code word for the 39ᵗʰ Regiment, Blue, the symbol for the 3ʳᵈ battalion.

Marshall and I found an unused hole with a cover of pine logs for a home. The hole leaked when it rained, but we remedied this by placing a transparent gas cape over the logs and covering it with earth.

Patrolling began almost immediately after our arrival. Most of it was routine, a series of daily patrols across a 400 yard gap between our right flank and the left flank of the 4ᵗʰ Cavalry Group. But Pappy, Kiser and Wright went on a patrol in front of K Company too, and Pappy shot a man, the first and only enemy casualty the patrol ever chalked up. He told us about it until we wanted to hear it no more.

Pappy, as the days passed, lost any popularity he might have gained when he joined the patrol. He was a squat little man with little steel-rimmed glasses, a lisp and thick lips, and he loved to talk. Because he was a Regular Army sergeant he believed himself senior to anyone in the patrol, even Hugel, who had been appointed our head by Lieutenant Saddle.

Hugel knew far more about combat. He had been fighting since Kasserine Pass, but he was not the kind of a man who commanded. He led. He would take his round body up front and trudge off through the woods while the rest of us trailed along behind, following more out of respect for his ability to stay alive than anything else.

Pappy, like many members of the old Regular Army, believed in the power of the spoken word, spoken often. He clashed frequently with Lieuten.nt Saddle, who he regarded with distain as a mere bother. The most serious of these arguments came during our only large-scale operation in the woods.

After a week of holding, the regiment attacked. We saw little of the beginning of the battle. It was only evident at the CP in little ways.

Prisoners began to come in small groups, herded by one or two Americans. A jeep with a radio was parked in front or the CP dugout. We stood about the jeep listening to the radio, trying to decipher the cryptic messages about was happening beyond us in the woods.

Early in the afternoon, Lieutenant Saddle sent all the forward part of the patrol, except me, into the gap between our flank and the 4th Cavalry. The men were equipped with a "walkie-talkie" radio. They were to warn of any infiltration into the weak spot in the lines by the Germans.

Late in the afternoon everyone returned, led by an angry Pappy. A long argument ensued. It seemed that K Company had not been warned of the patrol's advance in front of the line. Their mortars had fired on the patrol, slightly wounding Wright in the shoulder. Pappy had withdrawn in both fright and anger.

Lieutenant Saddle finally got him to go back into the gap again, just as evening approached. I managed to go along. I can only suppose that the lieutenant believe my glasses would not reflect any light at night.

We passed out of the lines through the flank outpost and into low scrub, dodged across an open field into a tall narrow strip of woods and then "swept it."

This was Pappy's idea. It would have been simple suicide had anyone been waiting for our return. We formed a skirmish line across the narrow belt of trees and moved through them down the slope of the hill for about 400 yards, snapping twigs and thrashing about.

When we reached a point near a field of more scrub, we stopped, or rather, Villegas stopped us. Long before the rest of us heard or saw anything, he halted, waiting. In a few moments we saw three men from the 4th Cavalry. They had heard our noise and wanted to know what we were doing.

We assured them we were friends and told them we would be staying the night in the field. Then, as they left, we set up at the edge of the woods. We had brought a light machine gun with us, and almost everyone, except Villegas, had some sort of automatic weapon. He clung to his trusty M-l.

Marshall and I went to the far right of our little line and bleakly considered the prospect of spending the night. Just as we were settling down we heard a great scrambling in the woods. Riesinger stood up and bawled out, "Who goes there?"

In the gloom we saw a figure come out of the woods into the field. He carried a huge white flag in his hand and was waving it as hard as he could. We beckoned him over. He was only a boy, 19, a member of a parachute regiment in the lines below us on the hill. He said he was Swiss. He felt neutral, and that was why he wanted to surrender.

I tried to question him in German, but about all I could find out was that he wanted a cigarette. After a short while Thorpe took him back to the battalion, and we again settled down to our vigil.

It was a long dreadful night. Marshall and I had brought neither blankets or raincoats. We agreed to take alternate turns sleeping, but I could not even close my eyes. Marshall managed to dose a little, but I could not even do that. A cold wind blew up the slope from the plain below. Showers of rain fell every other hour and soaked into our clothes.

I sat and stared at the dark and thought of all kinds of things. The darkness took on shapes that grew stranger as the night wore on. Figures danced in front of my eyes. I saw heads, faces, trees, lips, menageries of animals and then the dark again. I huddled on the ground against some wet leaves and grew stiff. I got up and slapped my arms together. I sat down. I opened and closed the latch cover of my machine pistol. Sometimes I talked to Marshall, but finally we were too miserable to do even that.

At last morning came. Over the hill behind us, self-propelled guns and artillery began to fire. We could hear the grumble of the guns, then the whisper of the shells and then we saw explosions on the plain below us. As the light grew stronger, the sun shone dull and red through a haze of dust and mist. The battle below us began again.

White German tracers looped through the trees and intersected with streams of red American machine gun bullets. Stray shots popped over our heads. Smoke shells began to explode on the plain as it became bright-er and we could see the figures of men running across the plain. The popping of the bullets above us seemed louder and we withdrew to the cover of the woods. Our mission had been accomplished and Pappy, still angry at Lieutenant Saddle, ordered us back to the battalion CP.

When we arrived we found everyone packing and preparing to move. We gathered our own equipment and walked back through the trees to Schevenhuette. That afternoon we moved to Jungersdorf, following behind the rest of the regiment as it swung in an arc around Merode. We stayed a night in a house with an infantry squad from the 3rd Armored Division. Marshall and I took over an upstairs bedroom, lugged a coal stove up from the first floor and installed it, collected coal briquettes and made a fire. We slept that night cozy and warm, side by side, in a big old-fashioned bed.

Outside heavy artillery shells zoomed in and exploded, but we were so tired we did not hear them. Each one though, I remember, sounded as if it was coming straight down the village street, yet none of them landed near us.

The attack progressed well and next morning we moved forward again, this time to a new village, Schlich. We boarded a truck in rare morning sunlight and for several miles we raced across the flat Rhineland, as level as a billiard table, until we reached the town. It had been bombarded before being captured and one house was still burning. Many of its other buildings had been damaged.

In Schlich we had a whole house to ourselves. The rifle companies had already moved on to Derichsweiler, a mile farther across the plain toward Cologne, and were holed up, facing only the constant crash of artillery shells. We could hear the artillery fire all night long as it smashed into town. It did little damage. The riflemen stayed in the cellars of the big houses during the day and came out only at night.

Schlich was a looter's paradise. It had been evacuated before its residents had had a chance to remove much of their belongings. W had mattresses to sleep on, china plates to eat on, an alarm clock, paper to write letters and many other of the comforts of home.

During the first few days we threw the dirty plates out the kitchen window into a narrow passageway between the houses. Before long a shortage began to develop, so we were forced to wash them.

We had little to do while we were there. The front was static and few patrols were sent out. Instead, we explored.

One day Marshall and I walked out behind the village to find the dead German woman and her baby that Marshall had seen the day before. We were going to mark the place for a graves registration company but discovered that the bodies had already been picked up. Nearby, though, we found a complete range-finding outfit for a heavy artillery battery, in its cases and quantities of German ammunition.

Another day we went to the edge of Derichweiler with two men from the Ammunition and Pioneer Platoon to mark a road through the fields for the kitchen jeeps. It was a strange lonely feeling to be lost in so much space after the long imprisonment of the woods.

The next night I sat on the hood of the first vehicle and guided the jeeps up over this road. We felt our way along in the dark, guided by the burning buildings of Derichsweiler. All through the night we heard the explosions of shells in the town ahead of us, yet none ever struck near us. On the way back we picked up the bodies of three dead Americans and brought them back to battalion headquarters.

I had dysentery for two days from meat we had killed and eaten without aging. Fortunately I recovered rapidly after a visit to the first aid station where I received the traditional Army remedy, bismuth and paragoric.

Our food situation improved. We got 10-in-1 rations and cooked them on the stove in our house, supplementing them with what we could forage from the houses around us. I cannot remember now who was cook, but we had enough to eat for once.

Then, almost a week after we had arrived, we made ready to move again. The order came down one night and the next morning we woke to find the rifle companies already on the road returning from Derichsweiler.

Rumors had begun to circulate about an attack in the Ardennes. Lieutenant Saddle told us no one knew much about it, but it did not seem to be serious.

As we packed and loaded our trucks German planes appeared in the sky, for the first time in many months. Dogfights swirled over our heads and we stood in the streets of Schlich craning our necks to watch. It was the first time we were able to watch a battle without being a part of it.

Then we, too, began to move and before long we were swallowed up in a line of vehicles that stretched for miles along the road toward Eupen. Trucks, tanks, tank destroyers, jeeps and artillery traveled bumper to bumper. In Stolburg we passed through a check point looking for German paratroopers, and as we drove south into Malmedy Province, we met civilians hurrying westward. More and more troops appeared on the road. Big 90 mm. rifles were being, emplaced at road crossings and set up in fields. The shoulder patches of many divisions were mixed in the crowd — the 2nd, the 1st, the 78th, and the 99th. The Battle of the Bulge had begun.

11

By late afternoon we reached Sourbrodt, a small village west of Camp Elsenborn. We were returning to familiar country, the high Elsenborn Ridge near Mud Valley, our home before the move into the Rhineland. The 99th Division was in the woods about both Sourbrodt and Camp Elsenborn. We saw their black, blue and white checkerboard patches everywhere.

We drove through the camp, a former German artillery training center, and turned off the main road into the narrow valley of the Roer. The rest of the 3rd Battalion had arrived before us. The rifle companies were stationed in front of the battalion CP and the bare moor which had once been an artillery range.

We stopped just off the road in the woods and unloaded where once, more than a month before, we had seen a demonstration of how to attack a pillbox. We pitched the patrol tent beside the dirt road. The battalion was in reserve, while the rest of the 39th Regiment waited for the 99th Division to fall back through its lines. The "quiet" sector had erupted with fighting which was to be the battle for the shoulder of the Bulge.

That night we heard the icy crackle of artillery falling on the frozen ground touched with the remnants of November snow, but it seemed for away and we slept easily. The next morning we rode a mile and a half east on a dirt road to the rifle company positions. It was bleak and cold on the moor. There was nothing to see but the flat, gently rolling hills and the dark green of the distant pines. We talked to the men of Kiser's old platoon in K Company as they tried to dig in the frozen ground and were thankful that we could stay in our tent.

The battalion anti-tank platoon came by with its half tracks and emplaced its guns on the edge of a shallow draw to the K Company flank. The platoon commander told us L Company was far to the right front. We did not go to see them, instead we walked slowly on the muddy road, back to the battalion CP.

That afternoon a mimeographed sheet of paper telling the story of the Malmedy massacre was handed around and we began to realize how bitter the fighting was in other places.

Because we were in reserve, the patrol again had little to do. For several days our only duty was to act as a personal bodyguard for the colonel where ever he went and to ride on jeeps passing back and forth between the battalion and regimental CP's.

But on the third day of our arrival Hugel took six men and traveled in a wide arc in front of the battalion position. The seven men saw several self-propelled guns moving into position and heard the whistle of a German squad leader, but all returned to the tent unharmed. When they were back, Lieutenant Saddle told them he was surprised they had made the half-circle without incident, a remark which did little to increase his general prestige in the patrol.

Because there was nothing else to do, Marshall and I spent all one day digging a huge foxhole and then roofing it over with logs. There was no great danger that would cause us to use it, but the activity kept us warm and occupied. It was a nice foxhole; we slept in it one night and then abandoned it for the friendlier atmosphere of the tent.

That same day L Company captured a paratrooper, one of a number who had been dropped at the beginning of the battle. They had been badly scattered because they had been dropped at night, and most of them were captured before they did any damage.

Our paratrooper was all alone. He was not very bright and he did not have a very good idea of what he was supposed to do after he hit the ground, but Lieutenant Saddle, in his grandiose fashion, decided that he was something special. He had him brought to the patrol tent, fetched the battalion interrogator — a German-American named Fritz — and tried to question the paratrooper.

We sat around the trio in a lamp lit circle — the lamp having been borrowed from the battalion CP — while the interrogation went on. First, Saddle told the German to take off all his clothes. This was to make sure he had no concealed weapons, he told us.

Then he had Fritz ask him about his unit, his mission, and what he had seen before he was captured. The German answered all the questions with either a "ja", a "nein" or an "Ich weiss nicht."

At least, Wright said, "Give him a sock, Fritz."

"What do you mean? Hit him?" Fritz asked.

"Sure. Go ahead."

Fritz drew back his hand and slapped the prisoner gingerly on his face.

We could not help laughing, and our laughter was the psychological key to our intentions. The prisoner smiled, like knew we were only fooling. Lieutenant Saddle hauled out his pistol and dramatically cocked it and examined the chamber, but it was no use. The prisoner just would not be fooled. I doubt if he knew anything anyway. He was led away in triumph, while our intelligence officer took his lantern and went back to the CP to report failure.

On the fourth night after we had arrived in the Bulge country, we woke to the sound of feet moving past the tent. The Germans had attacked E Company of the 2nd Battalion to the left of our position and had broken through the line. The 3rd battalion had shifted into the hole during the night. The next morning it counterattacked to regain the lost ground.

The change in the position of the rifle companies meant that we had to move, too. We struck our tent and took it over a wooden bridge to the other side of the Roer, not far below the woods. This was the battalion rear, where the kitchens and supply dumps were kept. The rest of battalion headquarters and part of the patrol went up through the woods closer to the front.

Saddled as I was with the care of the patrol's supplies, I stayed at the kitchens most of the time. Each day I walked to the forward CP with mail and equipment. In the afternoon I came back and sat around the tent with those who had been left behind.

The road to the forward positions had once been liquid mud, but now it had frozen into a series of strange bumps, dips and curves. It was almost impossible to drive a jeep over it and I found it easier to walk the several miles.

At the forward CP—still more than a mile from the front—the patrol had found its way into three very fine foxholes. I spent a night in one with Marshall. It had been built with a very low ceiling so that it was just possible to sit up inside it, but it was dry, and it had a coal stove built into one wall.

We had left some coal nearby when we had camped in the area in November. Stoked with this, the stove gave off so much heat that it was comfortable to lie about in the hole in our shirt and trousers. We used gasoline for light again, but it was far from satisfactory.

The other holes were almost as well built. They had been dug on the edge of a large clearing in the woods, and I remember how the shone shone there on the day before Christmas. The cloudless sky was a brilliant lovely deep blue.

Through its icy afternoon light we saw huge formations of planes flying south. They were dropping supplies to the 101st Airborne Division at Bastogne. The planes looked like gold fish in a great blue bowl, each trailing a white vapor streamer behind it as it moved south.

On the same sunny afternoon, four of us made the only patrol where we received enemy fire. I say "us", for I had managed to sneak along. Marshall and I, Perez and Spooner were to go through L Company's line, down a hill to a point in a little valley. There we were supposed to find out what the small blob that Lieutenant Saddle had located on an aerial photograph might be. Saddle showed us the route to take and went with us as far as the L Company CP.

Saddle did not discover I had come along until after we had started. I was wearing green sunglasses too, which made him particularly unhappy, and he specifically ordered me to stay off any future patrols. I humbly agreed, and we continued on our way.'

71

We clumped up the frozen road in the sunlight, talking happily until we came to the Kalterherberg-Elsenborn Road. We crossed it and walked through the woods, over a light crunchy covering of snow, stopping for a moment to visit at the K Company mortar positions.

I remember someone told us that Lieutenant Toujay — the first officer I had seen in combat — had been badly wounded when a shell struck the K Company CP dugout.

Just behind the front line, the woods were low and scrubby, and we passed along a row of foxholes, calling to the men we knew until we came to the L Company CP. There we said goodbye to Lieutenant Saddle and went forward to the front line. The men in the second platoon were not happy to see us. They still resented the easy existence we had at the rear. I was surprised to find that many of the platoon had been wounded: Jones, the unhappy squad leader; an Italian we had known in Mud Valley; Arnolfo Flores from another squad, and several others.

Frank Santana, had been killed in Derichsweiler by artillery. He was the first man to die in the platoon after I came to it. I remembered him well because whenever hot cakes were served in Mud Valley he had always run to the chow line calling "Pine cakes! Pine cakes!"

Artillery was making holes in our ranks. The company position was on the forward crest of a hill and it was well known to the enemy. Each night, after the Cub artillery spotting planes went home, the platoon was shelled by German self-propelled guns. Two days before a German combat patrol had attacked the third platoon and two men had been killed.

I began to realize how much of the fighting we had missed by being in the patrol. It was dangerous while we were out in front of the lines, but we could always return to the comparative safety of battalion headquarters when we were through. The riflemen could only lie in their holes, shivering, and listen to the shells.

We told the men in the front line foxholes that we were going out for a walk in the woods. Then we set out across a wood road into the trees. On the other side it was sunny and still. The light flickered through the dark boughs and dazzled off the white patches of snow, but the woods seemed featureless and blank. We walked in single file, trying to keep the sound our boots from being heard.

We could see nothing and hear nothing. Even the artillery had stopped firing. Carefully we worked our way down the slope of the hill toward the creek bed. Spooner took the lead, then came Marshall, then Perez and then me.

At the bottom of the hill, Spooner edged out into a snow-covered field. Beyond it lay the creek. Across the creek another pine-studded hill rose. We did not speak, but moved using signals. We kept searching the trees, but we could see anything.

We crossed the edge of the field and entered the woods again. Up ahead I saw Spooner stop for a moment, look down, and then move on. When I reached the point where he had stopped, I found a brown German mine box beside the trail. It seemed a good time to stop to me, but Spooner kept going down the slope, steeper now, until he reached the bottom. Marshall moved to his right and together they peered out through the trees.

Suddenly we heard a shout across the creek and an

answering shout further up the hill to our left. Spooner turned and sprinted past us. Perez and I turned and followed him, leaving Marshall momentarily alone. Then he, too, joined the race.

We crashed through the trees. Their boughs lashed at our faces. The wind whistled in our ears. My helmet fell down over my eyes. Frantically I pushed it back up again. We heard the Pop! Pop! Pop! of a light mortar off to our left. Its shells exploded somewhere, but they were not very close. The fire was not repeated, and we did not hear any more shouts. Panting, the sweat running down our laces in spite of the cold, we finally stopped after we had gone 100 yards. I do not believe I have ever run 100 yards faster in my life.

After we had regained our composure and our breath, we circled slowly back up the hill, our caution lost, until we came back into L Company's lines again near the third platoon. Now we could begin to boast about the patrol. We were happy and in full sunlight as we went back down the road to the battalion CP.

12

It was the last patrol I made with Saddle's Rangers. That night I went back to the kitchens to watch over the supplies.

Marshall stayed forward and during the next two days he and Kiser and Hugel made a patrol every day in front of L Company, trying to locate an enemy outpost. This strong point was somewhere in the woods not far from the line. From it, the Germans had direct observation of the Eisenbrn-Kalterherberg Road, and Colonel Stumpf, the battalion commander, wanted it removed. He also wanted a prisoner, and when continued patrols failed to provide one, he called in Lieutenant Saddle.

That night Marshall, Kiser and the rest came back down the road from the forward OP with bad news. The patrol was to be disbanded.

We were told the rifle companies were short of men and because of this we were being sent back to our own units. This was true, but there was more to it. We had taken it much to easy and we had failed to convince the colonel that we were really necessary. We had no excuses, and we did not look forward to returning to the front lines. A gloomy group of men went to bed that night.

The next morning we turned in our supplies to the headquarters company supply sergeant—who took them with ill-concealed glee—and drew rifles from L Company again. Mine, I remember, was almost rusted shut and I had to fire a round through it to clean it.

Then Marshall and I, Hugel, Spooner, Ellis and Pelky hiked the long three miles back to the company and reported to the second platoon.

13

That day I experienced a feeling that I would have for the rest of the war each time I returned to combat. It was as if I was on a stream, in a boat moving toward an unseen waterfall. I could hear the thunder and power and dread of the waterfall ahead of me, but I could not see it, and I was unable to escape from the river.

The waterfall was death and the river was time and I was caught in the boat by a superhuman force which would not release me. When an attack was over, or when we withdrew from the front line to return to reserve, I felt as if I were being pulled back to the safety of reality, to a land which, while it was alien, was human, and therefore not strange.

Each time I went back into combat I took on my shoulders this feeling of dread. It was often like an actual weight and as time passed and the war progressed, it became heavier and heavier. I hated to be afraid, yet I could never completely overcome that fear. It is all very well to point out that it makes little difference whether one is afraid or not. Death comes to everyone sooner or later, but the preservation of self has automatic responses in the body and it can never be completely overcome.

Yet sometimes death did seem a friend, as I have said before. I formed a simile in my mind about it, thinking of it as a figure just beyond a dark pane of glass which I was never able to penetrate.

In the country of combat the senses became acute. Time telescoped itself into a tiny fraction of the normal unit of man's thought — a day — and then strangely expanded in retrospect, so that finally all my time at the front seemed to be one long existence, shadowed and lightened by daylight and night, but which was neither darkness nor day.

I wanted to draw back from a return to the front line, and it was with fear and loathing that I came back to the second platoon.

The first squad had been even further reduced by shell fire since my last visit. Only Munk, Duplessis and Dumas were left when we arrived at the line of foxholes in the woods. There was no squad leader, but Percer had put the three remaining men under the control of another sergeant. Even Lieutenant Belt was gone. He had been wounded by shrapnel, and a Lieutenant Ross had taken his place.

Marshall crawled into a big hole with Munk and Dumas, while I got into another with Duplessis. He was a French-Canadian boy from Bath, Maine. He did not speak English very well, and I believe now it embarrassed him to be in an army in which he could neither understand very well, nor make himself articulate. In the Huertgen Forest, he had spoken to almost no one. I had exchanged only a few words with him until one night, by chance, we happened to be on outpost guard together.

We stood looking silently at the blank wall of the night for fifteen minutes and then suddenly it was as if a floodgate had been opened. He told me about his home, his family, his girl, French Canada, what he liked and disliked about his present position, everything.

After that we were friends, although he did not think Marshall and I had showed much sense in volunteering for the patrol. I was happy to see him again. I liked to listen to him talk. I crawled into his hole, a low shallow one, only two feet deep, roofed over with cut logs and open at both ends. He explained it had been closed at the rear, but after a German combat patrol the week before, he had cut the other end open to get free "if I have to get back."

Sergeant Jones had been his companion in the hole until Jones had been wounded. Between them they had racked up a stack of fifteen hand-grenades in adapters for the grenade launcher that Jones carried. These were piled at the front entrance of the hole. Now, however, Duplessis had been handed the BAR—which he did not think much of—"no damn good," he said. This rested at the other side of the low firing port at the forward end of the shelter.

Evening approached and it was soon cold. I lay on my stomach on some pine boughs in the bottom of the hole and shivered. We talked about what had happened during the time Marshall and I had been away. Duplessis toll me about the attack on Derichsweiler. "We ran all the way across the plain," how Santana had been killed and how the New England Italian, a friend of Dumas' had been wounded in the head and how the Italian thought he was dying and had given away all his personal possessions before they took him back to the aid station.

As soon as dusk fell, the Germans began their artillery barrage. As we lay in the unyielding earth of the hole, we could hear the faint sound of the guns over the hill in front of us as they fired, a clap-bang, as if someone had dropped several books on the floor. Then there was a wait of several seconds and the shells whistled in and exploded in the trees. Twigs and branches snapped and fell after the sound of the explosions died away. We could smell the cordite. A shell would go over the hole, to the right, over, in front and then over again. It was a long wait as we heard the sharp, high whistle that grew and grew in intensity and then shrieked down and buried itself in the earth.

I continued to lay on the floor of the hole and tremble. It was from both fear and cold.

After fifteen minutes the barrage stopped. Marshall got out of his hole and crept across the ground to ours.

"You okay?" he said.

'Yeah," I said, sounding braver than I felt.

We agreed we would check on one another in alternate trips after each barrage. Then he went back to his hole.

A few more shells came crashing down, splintering limbs and snapping off pine branches. I scuttled over to the other hole to find everything was all right. Then the barrage was over and it was night. Out in the darkness snow began to fall, a feathery, light drift of flakes. Duplessis and I lay down in the hole and tried to sleep, but it was getting colder and we were able only to doze.

An hour passed and Percer came fumbling his way along the line in the darkness.

"We're going to be relieved about one-thirty," he said. I felt a great burden slip away. Our positions were to be taken over by a company from the 60th Regiment.

"You and Marshall stay here until they come up," Percer said. "You're part of the covering forge."

We were part of a series of outposts left behind as most of the company dropped back into reserve. Marshall and I were to take the BAR and remain in

Duplessis' hole until the 60th men came to relieve us. Two men were being left in each squad, although this did not mean much. All squads were under strength.

Several more hours passed, interrupted now and then by fire along the line. Since the German combat patrol of several days before, the company kept a quick finger on its triggers. Just after midnight Percer and the runners came by, collecting the rest of the platoon. Marshall moved over to my hole.

We were now bothered by the thought that perhaps the Germans might choose this time for another attack. We kept searching the woods in front of the hole for signs of movement. Because we were tired and sleepy, we sometimes thought we saw something, but we were now not as trigger hapy as we might have been. I only fired once—at nothing.

No one came to find out what the shot meant. Time dragged on. We began to feel more and more alone, isolated from the rest of the war by the wall of falling snow and the darkness. Then at 1:30 we heard the sound of men behind as and in a few moments we turned over our hole to two soldiers from the 60th Regiment.

We walked slowly back through the snow, now several inches deep. The rest of the covering force had assembled at the company CP under Sergeant Cogborne, the regular Company L first sergeant. He had been wounded in Normandy—one of four times he had been wounded—and he was on to return to the United States on a rotation furlough.

Through the darkness and the new soft snow we marched back along the road through the woods into reserve. It was a miserable march. Our trousers were wet after a short distance. Then we came to the dirt road, which ran across the highway into the reserve area, and discovered it had iced over. A smooth coating of ice, as slick as glass, covered each rut and rise. It was almost impossible to stand up or maintain any kind of pace. We slipped and slid and cursed. Now and then someone would fall with a crash to the ice, filling the air with obscenity. The men nearest to him would help him to his feet, often falling themselves and we would walk on. It was long after two o'clock in the morning before we finally reached the reserve area.

We had expected to take over some dugouts left by the 60th, but instead we swung off the road into a grove of thin pines carpeted with nothing but snow. We could only stand around, swear, and wait for morning to come so we could better our plight.

When morning finally arrived, we found we were in one of the old areas left by the Second Battalion of the regiment during our previous stay at Mud Valley. Here and there among the trees were the remains of shelters. Some were only holes in the ground. others were lean-tos or tiny low huts. Marshall and I made for a hut as soon as it was light enough to see where we were going, only to be evicted by our former patrol commander, Lt. Saddle.

At last, Marshall and I found a small hole, half-filled with snow and partly covered with boards. During the morning, we improved its roof and hiked three-quarters of a mile through the trees to Mud Valley. There we found a tiny coal stove. We brought it back and put it in the hole, stoked it up and crawled into our sleeping bags. It had been 24 hours since we last slept.

When we awoke, it was supper time and the platoon was astir with the kind of activity which meant something was about to happen. It was always easy to tell this. The first sign was usually a runner from the company command post. He visited the platoon often, sometimes bringing mail, asking for certain individuals, to announce showers or that movies were waiting, or—very rarely—simply a social call. But usually he came to call the platoon sergeant to a company meeting. It was this summons we dreaded most. We would watch him—usually it was Murrow, a short man from the south—as he moved toward us, his face expressionless.

"Percer, they want you at the CP," he would say, or "All platoon leaders."

Murrow never knew any more than this. We would always question him, but we would have to wait until Percer came back before we knew what was to happen. Percer would tell the squad leaders and the squad leaders would finally tell us.

That night I felt, for the first time, that something was going to go wrong. As soon as I saw Percer come back from the meeting I knew whatever was to happen would be bad.

The orders finally reached us: a full company combat patrol into the woods in front of the line which we had just left. Its mission was to clear the Germans from the hill and keep from them observation of the Kalterherberg-Elsenborn road. The second and third platoons were to move abreast two hundred yards through the woods, make an arc and return to the lines. The 60th Regiment then would set up an outpost in the area we had cleared.

The patrol was to be preceded by an artillery barrage. We were to have three tanks in support. They would move down a fire break on the left of the area.

The first platoon and the fourth platoon, which had no use for its heavy weapons, were to be kept in reserve.

It sounded easy enough and someone said, "We'll be back in time for supper." But that night I went to bed with a feeling of impending disaster.

The next morning we had pancakes for breakfast. Someone cracked the old joke about "they never give us pancakes except when we're going to attack." We fell in at 9 o'clock and began to move up the road to the front. It was sunny, but warm only if you stayed out of the shade. The road was not so slick as the night before.

At 10 o'clock we reached the assembly area, just to the rear of the front line. There in the scattered low hardwood trees, we made final preparations for the attack. More snow had fallen during the early morning and covered the ground to a depth of almost two feet.

I had decided not to wear my overshoes. It was easier to move about rapidly without them and I knew we would be moving. But after a short while in the snow I began to wish I had brought them. The cold from the snow seeped up through my combat boots. I stamped my feet and knocked one shoe against the other to keep the blood moving.

At 10:15 the artillery began. Shells fell first on the slope in front of the lines and then moved forward into the valley of the Schwalmbach. We heard the growling roar of tank engines on our left as the three tanks churned through the light snow. We waited tensely for a moment and then we moved off forward through the trees, past the foxholes now occupied by the 60th.

We ran across a wood road which ran parallel to the front and into the trees beyond it.

The trees, the hateful trees. I have always remembered them from that day. They were low and planted close together in regular rows. The branches of one tree almost touched those on the trees on either side. I could see only their dark green boughs, tipped with snow and Marshall to my right. Ahead it was only five feet to the next tree. As soon as we entered the woods we were caught and trapped in them. We could move only by passing orders from one man to the next. That was all we could see.

I looked to the right and moved forward to a tree. Marshall did likewise. Then I looked ahead and to the right. Marshall was gone. I hurried to the next tree and caught up with him. No one was on my left. Snow brushed off the branches as I passed between the trees and fell on my field jacket. My feet plowed through the snow. Soon my trouser legs were damp.

A mortar cough-coughed somewhere in the trees to the left and I pitched forward into the snow. The shells exploded behind me and I heard someone call out in agony as I crawled forward through the snow. But the mortar did not fire again and after a moment we were all up and moving forward again. A few more feet and we crossed a narrow path in the woods which showed signs of recent travel. A German telephone wire ran along its edge. I saw Percer slash it apart with his trench knife and then pass into the trees on its downhill side. The hill sloped gently toward the valley and the trees grew progressively lower as we traveled down until they were only as high as my head.

Then we came to a clear space between the plot of forest we had been moving through and a saw new group of trees. It was not really a fire break, just a space to designate a different planting.

I found myself looking with surprise down its line to find the rest of the platoon in sight. The word "hold it" came down the line and we stopped in the cleared path and squatted in the snow, too wary to sit down. It was quiet for awhile and then firing broke out on the left up the hill. It sounded American. There was no sudden rip, rip, as German machine-guns made, but only the steady tack, tack, tack of a Browning. A few bullets went over our heads, but they were high so we did not even duck.

I sat down in the snow and waited, a little calmer because nothing had happened. Somewhere in the downward attack, I had taken off the mitten on my right hand so that my trigger finger would be free. I had stuck the mitten in my field jacket pocket. Now it was gone and my hand was getting cold.

I looked for the mitten in the snow, but I could not find it. Finally, I gave up searching and tried to light a cigarette. To my dismay, I found my hand was so stiff from the cold I could not hold a match. I rubbed my fist against my clothes and after several tries finally got the cigarette lit.

The artillery had stopped and it was quiet again for a time. But I did not notice it because I was rapidly getting colder and colder. I began to shiver. Soon I was shaking. My teeth hammered together until I had to clench my jaws tightly to make them stop. I could feel each tremor begin deep in my body, spread through it, and then I'd be shaking and shaking until the physical effort of shaking created warmth and I stopped for a time. But then it started all over again.

I stood up and stamped my feet for awhile end flailed my arms about, losing in my discomfort any thought of watching for the enemy. But I soon grew tired of this and sat down and began to shake. The day passed, but I lost count of the hours. How long we remained in the clearing, I never knew, but it must have been a long time.

The sky clouded over. Now and then I'd look over at Marshall. Now and then we would curse, long, vehement curses which did nothing except to make us feel slightly better. Finally, Percer came down the hill with Lt. Ross and new orders. We were to swing around, face the hill and advance into the trees. Someone asked why we were doing this, but all we were told was that there was a German machine gun somewhere back in the direction we had come and we were to attack it. A light machine gun was moved into the apex of the slight triangle were formed and Lt. Ross said, "Run a belt through it."

We all fell in the snow after the first bursts of answering fire popped over our heads and Lt. Ross said, "That's enough."

We waited while Percer sent Ray McNulty's squad into the low trees. They disappeared almost immediately. Then there was a sudden burst of fire and they re-emerged, dragging two wounded with them.

After another long wait Percer and Lt. Ross returned.

"All right," Percer said, "We're all going in."

I was not sure what this meant but the rest of the platoon spread out to the right in a long line and we started up the hill. We had only gone a few yards when we heard shots at the right end of the line. Three more men were dragged out of the trees, one shot in the head, the other two wounded in the legs.

We began to fire blindly into the trees. Confusion burst upon us. I stuffed clips into my rifle and fired and fired, although I saw nothing in front of me. Spooner's rifle banged away and roared and roared into my left ear. Behind us Lt. Ross crawled through the snow as he shouted, "Fire and movement, goddamn it! Fire and movement!" Now and then he would punctuate this with shots from his carbine.

We moved a little, crawling forward in the snow, firing, stopping and then moving a little more. Duplessus was on my right. I could hear him cursing. His automatic rifle was filled with snow and had jammed and would not fire.

Suddenly I discovered I had only 16 rounds left for my rifle and I stopped firing, afraid I would run out of ammunition. Fire slacked off everywhere along the line as others faced the same predicament and we stopped moving about in the snow and just sat there, cold and frightened.

Then either by general order or common consent we began to retreat off the hillside, back to our former position. The attack had been a failure.

It was growing dark and my wet clothes had frozen. My feet were numb. All I could think of was a great desire to get off this hillside and back behind our lines.

For a long time nothing happened. At last we all stood up and slowly moved to the left, back in the direction we had come early in the morning. But our ordeal was not over. We were handed bandoleers of new ammunition. We waited yet again while Captain McClelland went back to consult with the battalion commander.

Finally he returned. The attack was over. We started back toward the 60th's main line of resistance where we had begun early in the morning.

We moved back across the trail we had passed. On one side there were two dead Germans and on the other a dead American, the sniper from our platoon. He had been killed by the mortar shells which had fallen behind me as the attack began. The Germans had been shot by a patrol from the platoon as it moved to capture the mortar.

One of the Germans had a splint on his broken arm, but he died before he was carried back to first aid. As we moved past him, someone reached down and un-buckled the man's wrist watch, I looked away.

Out on the wood road the company formed a line facing the woods and after much confusion prepared to go down the flank for another try at the German posi-tion. Just as we were almost ready to move, we heard, far away to the right, the hollow kachaf, kachuf of mor-tars and in a moment shells began to explode along the road. We plunged into the woods and lay in weary res-ignation, our faces in the snow. Harsh, grating voices whipped us to our feet end we began maneuvers in the darkness, always moving to the left, while somewhere the tanks edged forward, firing their machine-guns as they went. The red light of tracers shone through the trees. There were shouts on the left flank of the company.

I looked down at my rifle to find it was crusted with snow and frozen shut. Desperately, I worked the bolt back and forth, trying to get it into operation. Then we stopped and stood still in the darkness. We had failed again.

After that discipline and order broke down. It was now completely dark. You could only see the shapes of men against the white snow. Following each other, as sheep follow a leader, we went back out into the open space of the road and began to move back toward our lines. The tanks started to pull back too, and at the sound of their engines, German artillery, far across the valley, began to fire.

When we heard the sound of the shells leaving the guns we all fell forward into the snow and only the angry commands of the platoon guide got us to our feet. Half-running, we went through the trees toward the 60th's lines. The artillery kept pace with us, and the night was lighted with the flash of exploding shells. A great flash exploded near me, knocking me to the ground and I felt a stinging blow against my side. I lay senseless for a moment, certain only that I had been wounded. Then I moved my legs. They were all right. I felt along my side, found ripped cloth and the warm touch of blood and I shouted, "I'm hit."

Someone in the darkness called, "Heintze's hit." Further away, I heard, "Medic!"

I lay still for a moment and waited. No medic came.

Shells were still dropping around us. I did not want to stay where I was, but I felt I was privileged to have medical attention.

The man next to me – it was Fried – stumbled over me.

"Can you walk, Heintze?" he asked.

"I don't know," I said. "I think so."

I stood up.

"Come on," he said. Men were getting up and moving to the rear.

"Here, take this," I said as I gave him my rifle.

89

He took it, carried it a few steps and then threw it away.

We continued dodging through the trees in the darkness until we came to the rest of the platoon lying in the snow.

"Where is everybody?" someone said.

Neither Lt. Ross nor Percer were around.

"We're supposed to withdraw one hundred yards behind the line and wait," someone said.

"What for?"

No one knew. I was growing angry.

"I want a medic," I said.

"Is that you, Heintze?"

It was Marshall.

"Yeah, I'm wounded."

"Where?"

"I don't know. In the side."

We lay in the darkness for awhile and shouted several times for a first aid man, but none appeared. Through the trees a group of men came toward us. It was the fourth platoon. They, too, were moving to the rear. We watched them pass, but no one said anything. Just then Percer came back.

"Cone on," he said. "Let's get out of here."

Without a word, we trailed along behind the fourth platoon, back through the woods to the icy road we had passed the day before, slipping and falling as we went.

My side had begun to grow stiff. It hurt now and the

BAR belt I was wearing was rubbing against the wound. Marshall and I tried to get it off, but we could not release the catch. Percer fell behind to see what was the matter.

"I'm wounded," I said, angrily.

He was suddenly solicitous. "Here, I'll give you a hand," he said, and he put his arm around my shoulder.

"No, no, I'm okay," I said. "I just want to get this damned belt off."

He began to work at the catch. All three of us fumbled with it as we slithered over the ice. We were all groggy from the explosions of the shells and I suppose none of us knew exactly what we were doing. Finally, we got the belt off and threw it into some trees beside the road.

It was easier walking without the belt, but soon I began to limp. I was afraid I would fall on the ice and hurt my side. As we walked, Percer told us Kosik had been killed. It seemed a long way to come, all the way from Africa, to his death there in the snow.

It was two miles from the front to the Third Battalion aid station. I walked most of the way. Just before we reached it, a jeep came by and I hitched a ride on its hood.

The aid station was in a tent, pitched just off the road. I should have gone to the 60th's aid station, which was closer to the front, but I did not know where it was.

When I walked into the Third Battalion station, the medical officer looked at me and said, "What's your trouble?"

"I'm wounded," I said.

He found this difficult to believe until I told him I

was from L Company. Then he said, "You boys have been having a rough time. We've been packing you back all day."

He made me undo my trousers and looked at my wound. It was a large raw spot on my right hip, burned slightly at the edges from the hot shrapnel. The doctor covered it with a dressing and for the first and only time I felt faint. I must have looked it, too, for he quickly had me sit down and brought me the standard shot glass full of whiskey.

I drank it without really tasting it. Then I was hungry. Outside the rest of the company straggled in, dispirited and bitter. Some of the food which we were to have had when we got back "in time for supper" had been saved at the aid station for the litter bearers. From it I got several pieces of cake and some cold ham.

Then, after a long wait, I went out to the road with one of the aid men and climbed into the last ambulance. We drove slowly back to Sourbrodt in the snowy night. Now and then artillery boomed beside the road, but gradually it grew quieter and quieter. At the collecting station at Sourbrodt I walked about a little and talked to the chaplain. One of the medics offered me some hot chocolate and some cookies he had received in a package from home. I munched them gratefully and looked at the floor filled with litters.

Then I was loaded into an ambulance with Ellis, who had been in the patrol. He had frozen feet and a concussion. A slight noise would make him jump visibly.

Our next stop was the clearing station where I got a bowl of hot coffee and had my wound redressed. Then it was back into the ambulance again. We had now passed out of artillery range. It was silent except for the muffled sound of the tire chains over the snowy road.

Ellis had been placed on a stretcher at the clearing station end was carried away somewhere when we arrived at the Fifth Evacuation Hospital in Eupen. I never saw him again.

I was directed to a ward tent outside the main building of the hospital where I found half a dozen of the less seriously wounded men from L Company standing about drinking coffee and talking excitedly about the battle. They told me seven of our guys had been killed and 33 wounded. It was two o'clock in the morning and I was too tired to care. I found a cot, wrapped a blanket around me and fell asleep.

'14

After breakfast I was on the move again, this time to the Sixth General Hospital in Liege. I spent three days there, sleeping under white sheets in a warm tent with a cement floor. In the mornings V-l rockets came over and exploded near the hospital. One knocked the nurses' tent down one morning, but no one was injured.

My next stop was the Fifth Field Hospital in Tirlemont. It had been bombed out of Vierviers and had moved to a normal school in Tirlemont to re-equip and reorganize. While it was so doing, it operated as a convalescent hospital.

The school was a large brick building with a roofed-over central court. Each classroom in the school was set up as a ward, fourteen men to a ward. We slept on cots without mattresses. Our only worry was not getting enough to eat and smoke. Each day we received a ration of one candy bar and half a pack of cigarettes.

My great problem was the candy bar. I could never decide whether to eat it all at once or a little at a time, making it last as long as possible.

Our ward held a collection of a variety of ailments, most of them non-battle casualties. One man, a Texan named Jones, who had been a clerk in a replacement center message unit, had hemorrhoids. Each morning the doctor would hold a ward sick call and examine us. Each morning Jones was forced to take down his trousers and display his rear end to thirteen other men. Each time he did, the doctor, a dim-witted captain, would say, "We ought to do something about that." But it was two weeks before Jones was finally shifted to a general hospital for surgery.

Another member of the ward was from the First Division. He had managed to parlay a case of dysentery all the way back to England. It was, he claimed, incurable, the result of a fall into a New Jersey bog. I met him again in Liege before I went back to the front. He was still working his case with great success.

The ward boy was Johnny Romano, a San Francisco Italian-American, whose brother was a guitarist with the Bob Hope show. To prove this, Johnny once borrowed a guitar and sang for us.

John Durkin was also in our ward. He was a member of the first platoon of Company L and one of the more fabulous characters I met in the Army. He was six feet tall with a mop of red hair and was from Wilmington, Delaware. He had come overseas with me and had been wounded on New Year's Day, as I had been. A piece of shrapnel had struck him in the head and surgery was required to remove it from his skull — although the wound was not serious. This in turn, meant all the hair had been shaved from his head. I can remember him standing in front of the coal stove in the ward, his thin jaw working as he talked incessantly, his head bald except for a tiny red stubble.

Sometimes John and I would leave the hospital on three-hour passes and go to the main square in Tirlemont. It was a big wide place, covered with snow and lined with cafes. One of them, the Cafe Sport, was our favorite. It had 35 red leather seats, a shiny zinc bar and large plate glass windows that looked out onto the street. We would sit there and watch the big ABC (American, British, Canadian) trucks going through on their way to the front.

Carl F. Heintze

We went to the movies, both at the hospital and downtown where two of Tirlemont's theaters were reserved on alternate weeks for soldiers. Most of the troops in town were men from the British Second or the Canadian First armies on their way back from England. Only the hospital and a truck company were American.

I was in Tirlemont for two weeks before I was moved again. My wound had partially healed, but my recovery was not fast enough to please the doctor. He sent me back to the Sixth General Hospital in Liege for two days for heat lamp treatments. Then I returned to Tirlemont. Two days later I was marked for a return to duty.

On a cold miserable day when the highway was swept with blown snow, I joined a truckload of men going to Vierviers for movement to the front through the Third Replacement Depot.

15

Vierviers was like a town on the frontier. It was packed with troops, men from the replacement depot, VII Corps troops, troops from a VII Corps rest camp and supply and rear echelon men. Everyone walked about with rifles, pistols or carbines. Black marketeers and deserters slunk through the streets at night, there were occasional shootings and often less serious crimes. I was unhappy and lonesome.

I managed to pair off with another man from the second platoon who had been wounded on January 1. We were both assigned to the depot guard company. This meant we had nothing else to do but stand guard. We could not go outside the buildings of the replacement depot, however, unless we were under escort.

It was not unlike being in prison. I wished very much to get back to the 9th Division. The snow had begun to melt, although it was still very cold, the battle for the Ardennes was nearly over and it was obvious that a spring offensive would begin soon.

The division was the only home I had. It contained the only friends I knew. Still I did not look forward to more combat. There was now a difference. Before I had been wounded, I did not believe anything could really hurt me. But now I had been wounded and I knew the scales had been tipped slightly in the direction of death. The impervious confidence I had had before was gone. Then, too, the Ardennes campaign made it clear the war would not be over immediately. We would have to fight all the way across Germany. No one knew how long this would take, but in January 1945, it seemed long enough.

From Vierviers I went to a forward replacement battalion in an empty radio factory outside Eupen for three days. There my friend from the 9th injured his foot climbing aboard a truck and returned to the hospital. I never saw him again.

16

I returned to the division at its rear headquarters in Monschau. We slept for the night on the top floor of a large red brick textile factory. The following morning we rode over the flat plateau to the east. Almost all of the winter snow had melted, but the February sky was gray and it rained most every day. The country beyond Monschau was bare to the Urft River. Its surface was deceptive. It seemed almost as flat as the Rhine plain. Only here and there was it interrupted by forests of pine, all of them terribly cut up by artillery fire. There were a few villages about. All had been abandoned and ruined.

The battalion rear headquarters was in Dreiborn, a dreary little place of large, square, flat-roofed houses. The rifle companies of the battalion were three miles farther to the east in or near Morsbach, a town they had just captured. It lay on the other side of a north-south arterial highway. Beyond the village the plateau suddenly broke into deep canyons which dropped to the Urft. On the farther side of the river big hills climbed toward the sky again.

The truck carrying us forward raced across the open space from Dreiborn to Morsbach. It pulled up in a courtyard on the edge of the village just as an artillery shell exploded on the crossroads. The Germans had observation of the crossroads by day. Travel during daylight hours was risky, but possible.

I arrived just in time to find the company preparing to move to a hilltop to the right of the town. The battalion was in a holding position. One company was in

Morsbach as a reserve. The other two were on two great bluffs above the river. They spent one week on one hill, one week in town and one week on the other hill.

The forward companies were separated from one another by more than a mile. Each also was a mile from Morsbaoh. But the Germans were on the other side of the river and it was considered unlikely that they would attack.

Many changes had taken place in the second platoon while I was in the hospital. The platoon had a new platoon leader, Lt. Moxley. He replaced Lt. Ross, who was now company executive officer. Percer was gone, too. One of his old ailments had taken him to the rear for hospital treatment. He never returned to the front.

Marshall was now squad leader of the first squad. I wanted to be with him, but instead I was assigned to the third squad, led by Sergeant Ray McNulty. I did not know any of the men in it well, but McNulty was a fine squad leader. He was from Chicago, a devout Irish Catholic, several years older than I. He had entered combat in France and was one of the few old timers left from that period of the war.

I hesitate to use the word love in speaking of male relations, but Mac was one of the two men in combat whom everyone loved. Captain McClelland was the other. Mac always spoke quietly. I remember once he gave us his food when we had none of our own. His easy, calm made us willing to do anything he asked. I would have followed him anywhere.

The assistant squad loader of the third squad was John Esposito, an older man than McNulty and the father or three children. Jimmy Bruner, a huge Georgian, was the first BAR man. His assistant was Tracer. Tracer and Bruner were both only 18. Tracer was small and wore glasses even thicker than mine.

By this time we had two BARS in each squad. The second BAR man was Frank Gearheart. Fried was his assistant. They were inseparable companions, yet strangely similar in appearance and temperament. Both were tall and thin. Both had thin narrow faces and fair hair. Fried stammered. After awhile Gearheart picked up this speech habit.

Green was one of the two scouts and one of the more disagreeable men I met in the army. He slobbered when he talked, which wan most of the time. He complained frequently, was useless for much of anything and spent all his free time in reserve and some of it in combat looking for souvenirs.

Buck Miller had taken over as platoon sergeant. McNulty, too, was a non-com. The platoon runners were Dumas and Pelky and we had a new medical aid man, Broughy, who always kept coming back to us in the days that followed. He seemed as indestructible as other medics seemed prone to be injured. The platoon guide was Flattery.

Because the platoon was moving out that night, I had time only to repack my few belongings and get into the column. We left Morsbach after dark in a misty rain and walked on the highway to the crossroads, through another village and then down the slope of the mountains to the company position. All our supplies had been sent in at night because the road to the canyon was under observation during the day. No shells fell on us as we moved in, however.

The platoon position was a peculiar one. During the day it was spent in holes dig into the side of the canyon under trees. At night it moved out to the barren hilltop to occupy holes. Another platoon took over. Then we returned to the canyon. The canyon holes were not very good ones. We did little to improve them. Because I was the odd "new" man in our squad, I slept alone during the day in a tiny damp hole which was so constructed it could be entered only by lying down on one's stomach and crawling inside. One then had to turn over. Getting out was even more complicated.

I was very unhappy, partly because I was alone, but largely because I had no enthusiasm for returning to the front. I knew I would escape from the war now in only one of three ways: I could be wounded again, I could be killed or the war would end.

The days grew warmer. Even the nights were not as cold. It did snow, however, on one of the nights when we outposted the barren hilltop. A man named Bischoff and I were in the last hole in the series of outposts. Beyond us lay the unknown. The snow was heavy damp stuff which blew against my glasses and made it impossible to see. Bischoff also wore glasses. Before long it was too difficult for either of us to see so I decided to move to the next hole and find a replacement who did not wear spectacles.

I started to walk to the next hole. But I had only moved ten feet when I realized I was lost. For a moment I could not find my way back to my own hole. Around me was a ring of whiteness, the lighter color of the sky, the darker circle of the earth. I was lost.

Carefully, I moved in a circle over the ground in what I thought had been the direction from which I had come. Before long I stumbled into the hole where Bischoff was crouched under a blanket. I explained lamely what had happened. He did not show much interest. My second try also was unsuccessful. But the third time I started out I bumped into a man standing by the next hole. He was as frightened as I. He had not seen me coming.

Before I could trade words with him, however, word came down the line that we were pulling back over the crest of the hill to our daytime holes. I had only to find my way back to Bischoff to tell him to come with me.

After our week on the hill was up, we trudged back to Morsbach to take our turn living in town. Life in the village was not as peaceful as it had been on the hill. Each night the Germans drove a tank up to their side of the river and fired a quick barrage into the village. Then the tank retreated and disappeared.

Tracer, Bruner and I were at the town outpost guarding a long canyon that ran up from the river to town when the barrage was fired. All the rounds were direct fire and came in very fast. Halfway through the firing the telephone to the company command post was broken. As soon as the shells stopped I jumped out of the hole and ran down the break in the line. A cow had been killed by shrapnel and had fallen across the wire, breaking it. A wireman came back with me and repaired it.

It was the first time Bruner and Tracer had been under fire. They were impressed with the rapidity with which I got the wire back in service. But there was really nothing brave about it. I knew the shelling was over for that night.

Another night while we were at Morsbach, we hiked back across the plateau toward Dreiborn and ran a field problem, practicing night attacks for the coming advance toward the Rhine. Because of the lack of cover on the Rhine plain all attacks there would have to be started in the darkness.

It seemed silly to be playing soldier in the midst of war with the enemy only three miles away. The problem proved to be as confusing as a real attack and much less like a problem with all the corners neatly tucked in.

Near the end of our stay in the village, we moved up to the second, or left, hill and took our turn there. The hill looked down on a Nazi training school at Vogelsang, a big gray group of buildings on a bluff above the river. The 47th Regiment had occupied them.

Our hill was bare except for three cement pill boxes which had been converted into command posts for two of the company's platoons and company headquarters. Rifle positions hal been dug between them around the crown of the hill. Tracer and I had a hole which looked down on Vogelsang, but we could not see the river below us.

Because we were under observation during the day, we could not get out of our holes much. Occasionally a shell or two would come across the river from the German site and explode harmlessly. Most fell on the first platoon side of the mountain, although one did punch a hole in Tracer's canteen, left outside the hole one night.

As soon as it was dark the entire company would rise from their respective places and dash across the top of the hill with their mess kits for supper. Then everyone trotted back to their holes to eat. Luckily, during this mass migration no shells were ever fired or we might have had many casualties.

One day Bill Shaw, a new squad leader, but an old combat hand, took several of us on a patrol down the front face of the mountain through some woods toward the river. It was an uneventful patrol except that we had

the odd experience of walking around the crown of the
hill and seeing shells explode on its top above us.

17

Our week on the hill was cut short by orders to move. We turned our positions over to troops of the Second Division early one evening and walked back in the darkness to Morshach for supper. The chow line was set up inside one of the village houses to permit the cooks to use lights. We passed through the house, filled our mess kits and then went outside to eat.

In a short all three rifle companies of the battalion were meandering around the village, clanking their mess gear and talking. Those of us who remembered the nightly barrage ate quickly, washed our mess kits and prepared to move on. We had just managed to get on the road when the tank made its nightly appearance across the river. Our trip across the plateau to Dreiborn was rapid and we were all soaked with sweat by the time we reached the village.

We slept in houses that night at Dreiborn. Before dawn we loaded aboard trucks and set out for the north. We traveled most of the day, moving along roads broken and wet with the spring rain. Later that afternoon we came to almost the same spot in the Huertgen Forest where I had first entered combat four months before.

We camped in what was left of the woods we had crossed that day to reach Germeter. The trees had all been leveled by shell fire and now lay jumbled into great broken heaps. Only broken stumps stuck out toward the sky in an area which later was to be called The Wood of the Dead. The forest was the same gloomy green, but at least the sky was clear.

Someone had built crude log shelters in the area and we moved into these. On our first evening we discovered we also had camped in the middle of a battalion of 155 millimeter rifles. Occasionally one of these would give a great groaning roar and send a shell across the Roar River to the east.

One night a German plane flew along the length of the front just at dusk. A bright curtain of antiaircraft fire followed it as it moved.

During the day we trained and cleaned our equipment. There was little to do at night, but we were allowed to have fires.

Finally, on the fifth night of our stay, just before midnight, we were wakened as the 155 battalion joined in the 1,000 gun barrage which began the spring offensive of 1945. The concussion of the big guns shook the ground beneath us and the sky was made bright as day by the muzzle flashes as the cannon fired.

Late the next afternoon trucks backed down the muddy, sloppy road from Germeter and we climbed aboard.

For the first and only time that spring, we got a detailed plan of what was to come. We were to ride to the Roer River and cross it behind the First Division. During the night we were to pass through its perimeter and attack south to the town of Nidiggen directly across the Roer from our hivouack in the woods. L Company was to be on the left of the attack, K Company on the right, guiding on the riverbank. The first platoon was to be in reserve.

In front of Nidiggen were trenches in which some Germans might be found. Because of this an artillery barrage was to precede the attack. This was to lift and move into to after we started forward.

It seemed like a good plan and for once we were ready to attack. The company was nearly up to full strength, we had plenty of ammunition, our equipment and weapons had either been repaired or was new and we were rested.

Just as it was growing dusk, we climbed aboard the trucks. The road to the river ran through the edge of the Huertgen Forest. It was moonlight and as we drove through the remains of Huertgen towns, it was as if we were passing through a landscape which had been abandoned for years. The ruins of the buildings were pale and unreal in the half light. Pools of water stood in the shell holes and bomb craters. Now and then shells passed over our heads toward the German side of the river. There was no answering fire.

After a short time we rolled down out of the hills into the valley of the Roer. The river was rapidly losing its crest, produced by the opening of floodgates on the dams farther upstream, but it was still full. The moon shone on the muddy water, making it seem milky and soft. We unloaded in a narrow meadow near some railroad tracks and prepared to cross. The far bank was black, but a footbridge—just planks set on pontoons been built by engineers across the swiftly moving stream.

The company formed a long single column and moved across the bridge. On the other side there was a steep climb before we come out on the beginning of the Rhine plain. No one said anything and there was no sound except the occasional purring of a jeep engine and our labored breathing. We passed through a deserted village on the river bank and after a short march came to another town occupied by the First Division.

We moved off the road on the far side of town and spread out to get a few hours sleep before the attack. When we awoke the moon was gone and it was dark. We moved out of the village into an open field to wait for the beginning of the artillery barrage. Ahead of us lay the hill with its trenches. Beyond that was a low valley and then the town.

Promptly at first light the barrage began. Great flares of red and white blossomed on the hill. The sound of their explosions showered down on our heads. At a shouted command we rose to our feet and moved forward toward the curtain of flame.

As soon as we came to the top of the hill and the first trenches, the barrage lifted, as it was supposed to, but not before a short round fell on a squad of the first platoon, almost wiping it out.

We pressed forward, crossing the trenches, all of them unoccupied. We paused at the top of the hill. The wrecked buildings of Nidiggen lay below, outlined against the bursting shells. Red tracers from tank machine gun fire licked the broken buildings like the tongues of snakes.

Dawn began to break as we crossed the valley and entered Nidiggen. The barrage stopped suddenly, leaving the world strangely quiet with only the squeaky sound of tank treads and occasional shouts of men as they moved in and out of the first houses. We did not receive any return fire until we reached them. Then a shell exploded in one of the buildings, wounding Tracer in the hand.

We crept along the sides of the store house while a tank moved along the center of the street, keeping pace with us. Now and then it fired its machine gun, sending a lazy loop of red up the street into a house. We cleared that part of town, leaving us more or less in the open. As it grew brighter, the height of land that lay behind Nidiggen became clear and we were under German observation. The brighter it became, the more accurate was the German shell fire.

By the time it was fully light. We had reached the far corner of town, marked by a two-story stone house. In front of it was a road which led off across the plain and beyond the road was a high bank, part of an even higher hill. Men began to hunch up behind the house, because it offered the only cover. Soon parts of all three rifle platoons of L Company were around or in the building.

One of the tanks, which had been following us, moved through the backyard of the house toward the road. Just as it did I saw two mortar shells drop toward us, strike the ground and explode. In a few moments several more crashed nearby, wounding Fried, Spooner and several other men. Fried was struck in the shoulder by a piece of shrapnel which injured a nerve in his arm, but which did not break the skin. Spooner was more severely hurt. It was the second time he had been wounded. A piece of stone from the house struck my hand, numbing it for a moment and making it bleed slightly.

The shelling stopped the attack momentarily. More than half an hour passed before the company pivoted to the right and started for the higher ground above town. We dodged around a large bomb crater, ran across a road and then ducked under a low stone bridge and crept up a dry creek bed. As we did, the German shelling increased. Some of the shells were 120 millimeter mortar rounds, great chunks of metal that soared through the air like flying railway cars. They passed directly over the creek bed, bury themselves in the ground on the other side of the creek. Everyone except Esposito clung to the bottom of the ravine. He leaned back on the grass and looked complacently at the sky. He believed when one's time was due, it would come and he would not worry until that happened. Even a dud which screamed overhead and buried itself in a wall did not phase him.

We stopped again, supposedly held up by snipers at the head of the draw, and took shelter in a building facing a small apple orchard. Lt. Moxley, our platoon commander, went over the bank at the far end of the ravine. In a few minutes he was back, shot through the wrist. That was the last we saw of him, he was on his way to the rear and eventually to the United States.

Buck Miller took over command of the platoon. Slowly we inched our way up the draw into the houses beyond it toward a church on the hill. We did not find any German soldiers, but the shelling seemed to follow us as we moved from house to house. In one building the concussion from a shell exploding outside almost knocked me down the stairs into the cellar.

Each house was wrecked and had been looted by German soldiers. In every room was a pile of junk, broken plaster and glass, bedclothes, pictures, papers, the remnants of life, but without people.

Late in the afternoon the town was finally cleared. We began to collect ourselves for the night. But we were not through for the day. L Company was ordered to move south of town along the bank of the river. Two hills blocked the way, there. We were to clean them both off and halt on the second. Soon we were back in the trees again. It was the Huertgen Forest all over again, the same blank, frightening face of the woods, the somber darkness, the shuffle of dead leaves underfoot and the tension of waiting for rifle or machine-gun fire to break the stillness.

We moved around the slope of the first hill in a straggling line of squad columns, far above the bed of the river. It curled round the hill beneath us. Across the stream was a flat in which stood a village. A long column of smoke rose from a burning building in the center of town.

It was quiet in the woods although shells were still falling in Nidiggen. We could hear concentrations of mortars strike the houses, but they were not where we were so we did not care.

We circled the first hill and went down into a little valley that ran toward the river. Behind us and above us a rock jutted out from the brow of the hill toward the river, apparently a tourist attraction. An iron railing ran around its top. A patrol was sent to examine it, but found nothing.

We began to climb the second hill. It was a steep climb. As we struggled upward, Gearhart hooked the trigger of his BAR in a twig and fired a single shot. Luckily, he had the gun at sling arms and the round went off harmlessly. Put it impressed Esposito who kept saying over and over, "Damn fool, almost killed himself. Almost killed himself."

As we neared the top of the hill the trees grew thicker. It also had grown dark and we had trouble keeping in contact with one another. Firing broke out somewhere on our left. It was irregular. Tired as we were, we did not pay much attention. At last we reached the top of the hill and halted by a wooden summer house, waiting for orders. The first platoon was somewhere ahead, but we could not see them in the rapidly approaching darkness.

Beyond the house was a small knob, covered with pine trees. It blocked the view into the next valley. The area was sprinkled with summer homes. Another stood off to the right. The first platoon had set up their command post there.

After a long wait, Lt. Ross came down to talk to Buck Miller. The first platoon, he said, had run into Germans on the other side of the knob and had been fired upon. We were to go round the near side of the knob to assist them. It was a cramped place in which to maneuver. The hill sloped off to the left, the knob rose to the right. The knob was so steep it was almost impossible to stand on its slope.

The first and second squads moved down the slope into the trees and disappeared. We started along the edge of the knob toward a clearing. We could just make it out in the gloom. Soon we could see another summer house. When we drew close to it Esposito threw a grenade at its entrance. Almost at once this was answered with a shot that passed over his head and I heard him yell. He turned back toward us and ran a few steps just as an enemy grenade arched through the air and exploded near him. He pitched forward on his face, with a peculiar grunt, dead.

It was obvious we were getting nowhere. It was now so dark we could not see anything, but behind Lt. Ross had taken on his usual chant, "Move up, God damn it, move up!"

Instead we began to back down from the knob toward the flat from which we had come. I heard more shots and someone's desperate shout, "Medic! Medic!" Then there was silence. The shout had come from Gearhart. He had gotten to the front side of the knob near the first platoon positions and had been killed by a burst from a German machine gun.

Discouraged and broken over the loss of the two men, we crawled back to the summer house and set up a perimeter defense around it. We were ordered to keep one man awake in each hole, but we were so tired we soon found we could not stay awake. Bruner and I dug a shallow hole and lay down. Through the night we dozed and woke at intervals, in a continuous nightmare.

Sometime during the night I heard the sound of an American barrage coming over the river. It must have been on a target mission. It sounded like the roll of a kettle drum—as steady and sustained as if a single artillery piece had been fired as a machine gun.

Before dawn we moved down off the hill, back toward town. As we felt our way back through the woods the Germans fired mortars into the trees, but most of the rounds fell far away. Not until we crossed the second hill did they come close. Then one large flat piece, almost spent, broke Munk's arm. I was happy to see him go and happy he'd never came back.

Back in Nidiggen artillery and mortar shells were still exploding, but the fire was not as heavy as the day before. We took shelter in several houses and tried, without success, to find something to eat. We had not had any food since the previous morning. We were also out of water and none seemed available.

After a long delay we shifted across town to another building and then began marching to the rear along the road we had entered Nidiggen on the morning before. We passed companies of both the 60th Regiment and the 78th Division. Before the town had been empty, now it was filled with troops, all moving forward to the attack.

114

No one seemed to know where we were supposed to go and we were all growing increasingly hungry and thirsty. We began walking through a shallow valley, but after we had gone a short way a mortar shell exploded ahead of us. We retreated and marched farther west toward the river.

After a long time and many dips and swales of the Rhine plain, we came to a village and stopped by a running stream to fill our empty canteens. Rations also were distributed. Late in the afternoon the sun came out and for the first time in several months it was really warm. The roads were beginning to dry and walking in overshoes, which I had worn since October, was difficult and seemed, for the first time, to be unnecessary.

Toward evening we came to a shallow valley through which ran a small stream. Low woods grew along its farther slope. We were to spend the night here though we were, practically speaking, lost. We did not know which direction the enemy lay nor where we were. The situation had degenerated into an uncertainty which remained for most of the war. We privates did not know where we were or what we were to do. From that point on everything that happened seemed to be improvised. The careful briefing we had received before Nidiggen was the last fully detailed report for an attack we would ever get.

We crossed the stream, set up positions, and a line that ran along the rear edge of the woods. Everyone began to dig, but we were all so tired we did not dig far. Bruner and I had scooped out a shallow hole by the time dark arrived. It was not deep enough to give much protection but we lay down anyway and fell into a fitful sleep.

Sometime later in the night artillery began to fall somewhere in the woods nearby and we wished we had made the hole deeper. Bruner tried to squeeze his big body farther down into the shallow depression. "Man, I really hate that artillery," he kept saying.

After a few haphazard rounds the firing stopped and we dozed off again, only to be wakened in the darkness by the familiar chant, "Get it on, we're moving out."

Still half asleep, we picked up our few possessions, formed into ranks, and began to move down the road once more. There was no moon. We walked along under the stars, staring at the lighter dark of the sky, trying to make out some form in the strange fields around us. The land was vaguely hilly. We passed a place where square box mines had been removed by engineers and stacked beside the macadam surface of the highway. Then the column turned off into a field. We could feel the rough contours of plowed ground and the wind blew through the dried husks of potato plants and sugar beets.

Behind us we could hear the squeak and rattle of tank treads. On and on we went. It seemed we had been walking for years, that the stars would never go out and the day would never come. Finally the land dipped down and ahead of us we saw the dim shape of a village. It was Ginnick.

As we came down the hill, we could hear a dog barking. I suddenly wished he were closer so I could throttle him into silence. Just as we reached the edge of town a great ripping roar like the sound of a gigantic piece of canvas being torn apart by the wind split the night and a shaft of yellow light flashed over our heads and burst on the lead tank at the top of the slope. It was followed by a cascade of sparks and a second zip-crack as another armor piercing 88 millimeter shell went into the earth.

The tank backed up the hill with a bellow of startled sound and rage. We fell to the muddy ground near some foxholes dug by the village Volksturm at its edge. When I rose to my feet, I discovered to my horror that the flash hider on the BAR I was carrying had become clogged with mud. Hurriedly, I cleaned it with my finger.

The Germans stopped firing after two rounds, but a German machine gun on the hill to the left of town now began to sound off. Its bursts were without tracers and we could not tell where they were coming from. Apparently the Germans had guessed, incorrectly, that we were beside the tanks, instead of in front of them. They continued to fire as we hurried to the shelter of the village. After a minute or two, the machine gun stopped too, and there was silence.

The village was long and narrow, as so many German villages are, and the houses were scattered along a single road with only a cross street or two. The road or main street ran opposite to the direction in which we were moving.

We were the reserve company. I and K Companies entered the village from the right, farthest from the hill. We moved to the left and began searching through houses on that side of town. We fumbled through two barns before we finally found an inhabited house. Inside was a single German soldier, a frightened old man and his wife and their two grandchildren. The soldier told us nothing except that soldiers had been in the village that afternoon. He could not or would not make clear why he had remained behind. The rest of the household was too frightened to talk, a clear sign that soldiers were not far away.

We left the house under guard and stumbled down the dark street. As it grew lighter, we came to a corner where the street intersected with the single main street. While Mac and the rest of the squad went on around the corner, Crosby and I poked into a barnyard enclosed by a wall on the side nearest the street, a big house with one of its walls blown down. Beside it was a concrete barn.

Curious, I walked into the house and lit a match. Just as it burst into flame, I heard Mac yell through the door on the other side of the house, "Drop it, damn it, drop it!" There was a yellow flash as a grenade exploded in the street. Men began to run past the wall outside the farmyard.

I turned and went back into the farmyard. More men were going by the gate through which I had just come. I scuttled across the yard into the cement barn and peeked out one of its tiny windows. Crosby followed me.

"Where is everybody?" he said.

"I don't know, " I said. I stood frozen by the window.

He ran out the door and moved toward the far end of the yard, lost in darkness. Just as he got to its low wall, he saw a German setting up a machine gun atop it. Both he and the German yelled at each other in German. Then he turned and ran back into the barn where I was standing.

Another German in the house across the farmyard said, "Hi,ya, bud," and threw a grenade at Crosby. It exploded but Crosby was not hit. As he came into the barn, Crosby said, "We're trapped!"

I did not say anything for I had just seen a squad of black-helmeted German paratroopers running across the intersection of the two streets. They had come down

118

off the hill above town to meet us in the village. Because we were nearest the hill, they had reached us first.

Crosby and I crept back into the barn and looked for a place to hide. My mind went blank. Everything had happened so rapidly, I could not think. I leaned my BAR against the wall and then stiffened with fear as I heard the sound of boots on the fallen tiles outside and the whispered sound of German voices.

"Isn't there any way out of here?" Crosby whispered.

Slowly, like a man in a sinking submarine, I felt my way along the concrete walls, but there was no rear exit. The wall was two feet thick and except for two small barred windows near the door facing the farmyard, it was solid and blank.

"We're trapped," Crosby said again, somewhat un-necessarily, I thought.

I hissed at him to be quiet. We could hear the pow-pow of American M-1 rifles being fired in the distance. The Germans whispered together again and then there was an explosion as they fired a Panzerfaust rocket over the houses like a mortar.

Gradually, it grew lighter and we could see we were in a sheep barn. Cement posts stuck up out of the floor at regular intervals. In between them were thick wooden doors. We carefully crawled back into the stall farthest from the door and sat down on the straw.

I tried to calm myself long enough to consider what to do. I came up with three possibilities. We might get captured—if someone came into the barn and found us. If they did not, we could wait for nightfall then try to escape into the fields and our own lines. Or we could wait until the company recaptured the town again. The last situation seemed the most likely.

119

I found myself wondering what I would do if I were a German paratrooper and I had just come through the door. Then I remembered that I had left my BAR resting against the wall outside. Carefully, I eased out and pulled it back into the stall.

Time passed. The sun came out and disappeared. The wind blew against the shaky timbers of the house across the street and made noises which sounded like feet walking across broken tiles. Mortar shells fell somewhere near us. Once we crept to the window and saw red American tracers flashing down the street.

I dozed for awhile, then I opened a K ration, took out a candy bar and ate it. The forenoon passed into afternoon. We heard German voices no more. Then gradually we became aware of the sound of M-1s down the street.

We went back to the window and in a few moments a brown field jacket flashed in the house across the yard. It was Pancho, a sergeant from the first platoon. We yelled at him to warn him that we were Americans, not Germans, and then we ran across the yard into the house and pounded him happily on the back.

"Where's the second platoon?" I asked. He did not know exactly, but he thought they were somewhere behind him.

Crosby and I finally found the platoon in a barn, stretched out on some bales of hay. Not many were left. Almost everyone had been wounded and one man, a tall blond fellow named Jensen, had been killed.

We found out that after the grenade had exploded everyone had run back down the street into a house. Then they had climbed out a rear window one by one and taken shelter in the foxholes on the edge of town. There the Germans on the hill kept them pinned down for the rest of the day. Jensen, who had been in the same hole with Marshall, had been shot through the head.

Only Mac, Crosby, Green and I remained of the third squad. There was only enough of the platoon left to form two understrength squads. Buck Miller had been wounded in the ear and Flattery had taken over command of the platoon. Marshall was now a squad leader as were Clow and Mac.

The German counterattack soon broken down and the first platoon began to push them back, reaching the edge of town by rushes, and cleaning out houses as they went.

We followed behind them. In one house we found a machine gun squad, their gun and two full boxes of ammunition. In another were several wounded men and a medic who had stayed behind to care for them. The rest of the paratroopers and the German tanks accompanying them had pulled out and were retreating across the plain toward the Rhine.

Our combined squads found a potato cellar and had just bedded down for the night when we were ordered to go pick up Jensen's body which was still in the foxhole at the edge of town. Ordinarily this would have been left to the cooks or Graves Registration to do, but on this one occasion we had to do it. I never learned why.

We stumbled through the dark streets until we found the company command post, picked up a litter and then carried the body back to town.

When we returned to the platoon, we learned from

Flattery that Duplessis had been killed. He had been burned to death in a tank destroyer. It was the last blow of a terrible day. I don't remember any other single night when I was so miserable in spirit. We had all liked Duplessis.

The next day we saw the tank destroyer, charred and desolate in the middle of the main street. Duplessis had volunteered to ride it as a guide toward the barn where Crosby and I were hiding. Just as the tank destroyer neared the street crossing a German leaned out of a second story window and fired a Panzerfaust through the open hatch of the tank, exploding the ammunition beneath its floor. The driver and the assistant drive got out, but everyone in the turret, including Duplessis had been burned to death. We could not even find their dogtags. The man who had fired the Panzerfaust also had been killed. He had fallen into the flames, only the metal hobs of his boots remained.

Duplessis was posthumously awarded the Silver Star, small enough a reward, it seemed to us.

18

The next morning, a sunny day, we climbed aboard trucks and drove forward, looking for the front. During the night we had been "pinched out" by other units and the fighting had moved far ahead. Few natural obstacles now lay between us and the Rhine.

The land was as flat and as featureless as a piece of paper. The only irregularities were villages, set a mile or two apart in the fields. The lack of cover between them made it necessary to attack at night or in the early morning and from Ginnick until we reached the Rhine almost all attacks began in the darkness.

That day we rode through several villages before stopping late in the afternoon at a crossroads with a few houses, a few trees, a church and that was all. Several miles away on our left we could see a great line of olive drab vehicles moving slowly eastward. It was the van of the 9th Armored Division, moving ahead of the infantry.

We formed a perimeter defense around the crossroads and began digging holes in the south earth of the potato fields. While searching for positions we found an abandoned German antiaircraft gun. Near it was a dugout its crew had built underground with a glass window, bunks and a stove. The platoon command post moved into it, marking one of the few times it was in front of the squads.

Early the next morning, while it was still dark, we loaded aboard trucks again and drove ten miles to the east to reach the village of Thum.

Thum had been bypassed by the armor. We had to

search the houses before dawn. We found no soldiers, but none of the civilian population had been evacuated. It was the first village we occupied in which this was true. But from then on almost all towns we entered had not been evacuated. The war had moved too swiftly for this to be done.

The third squad moved into a house near the center of the village. A small former soldier named Willi Schmidt, his wife and his mother were staying there. They had taken cover in the living room and the bedrooms on the second floor. They were all sleeping on mattresses on the floor when we arrived.

What to do with the Schmidt family became a problem. First, we had Grandma peel and cook some potatoes and fry them for our breakfast. Then one of the members of the squad found a large bottle of new wine which we sampled — with Willi's reluctant permission. After that we moved into the upstairs bedrooms and the living room, dispossessing the Schmidt family completely.

The company had been ordered to evacuate the entire village, collecting the civilians at the village church. This produced considerable argument from Willi who did not want to go anywhere now that the war had passed him by. But finally he and his family collected a great bundle of possessions and reported to the church.

Periodically, however, Willi kept returning to the house for something he had "forgotten." These frequent visits were embarrassing to us for we had begun going through the house. One such visit found us looking at a photograph album of his. Willi took this in good part, showing us a picture of him when he had been a member of a flak battery in Russia. He subsequently had been wounded and sent home to work on his farm. But he was less happy when one of the members of the squad killed one of his chickens and stewed it that afternoon.

19

We remained in Thum for two days waiting for the armor to take some high ground to the east. Most of the time we rested, wrote letters and stood outpost guard.

This outpost, like so many which were to follow, was a farce. It was in a roofed-over shed to the left of town among some bales of hay. A telephone line was strung from the shed to the company command post. It would have been of questionable value in an attack.

On the night of our second day in Thum, we started forward again, walking through the rainy night to Berkum, the next village.

Berkum was a railway stop which had been captured by the first battalion. The third squad occupied a warehouse north of the railroad station. It was a big barn like building isolated from the rest of the village. We found it was safe to move about in the open and we began to poke about.

I was searching two houses near the warehouse that faced the open fields to the east when a German woman excitedly told me that two soldiers were nearby. Cautiously, I walked around to the front of the house to find two artillerymen trying to hide in her front yard. Neither were armed and both seemed embarrassed, but happy, at being captured so easily. I took them back to the company command post.

There two other prisoners had turned up. The first sergeant told me to take them to the regimental prisoner of war collecting point in a nearby village. I borrowed a submachine gun and looking as fierce as I could, I walked them back down the road. They insisted on walking with their hands above their heads, although it did not matter much to me. All four were happy to be captured and laughed and joked among themselves as we went.

By the time I got back to the warehouse, the sun had come out and it was a brilliant early spring day. We could see another town a mile across the fields. On a road to our left front K Compny was trying to move forward to take it. Air bursts of artillery exploded over their heads as they went slowly up the road, taking shelter behind mounds of sugar beets.

The battle died down in the afternoon and we had nothing to do but sit on the loading dock of the warehouse. Toward evening it began to cloud over and by nightfall it was raining lightly. At 10 o'clock that night we marched to K Company's town and spent a few hours waiting in a large barn. Then at 2 o'clock in the morning we started off with tank support for the next town, Strassfeld.

The attack was so organized that the infantry moved along both sides of the road while the tanks drove down the roadway. I remembered with misgivings the artillery fire the tanks had drawn at Nidiggen. But nothing happened, except that confusion reigned in the darkness.

We stumbled about in the buildings, bumping into one another, cursing and trying to find doors to open. It was a black night without stars and the village turned out to be much larger than we had expected. It was morning before we had completely searched it. Our only opposition was three civilians who had been handed a machine gun by the departing German troops and told

127

to man an outpost at the edge of the village. They had wisely decided not to fire the machine gun.

A cold drizzle fell all during the night. Just before dawn the third squad was sent to set up a lonely outpost in a shed far to the north of the village. At first, we simply stood in the rain by the intersection of two barbed wire fences, but after a half an hour of this we took shelter in the shed. When it grew light, we returned to find the 60th Regiment moving through town. Marshall and I found a few men who had come overseas with us.

We went exploring and climbed to the top of the village church steeple, but the low overcast made it impossible to see anything. That night we received the first batch of replacement since crossing the Roer. Three of them were assigned to the third squad — Wagner, a frail little dark man; Sgt. Ernest Kalman, a Hungarian-American from New Brunswick, New Jersey, and Irving.

Irving was the most interesting of the three. He was short and stocky with a jutting lower lip and glasses so strong they magnified his eyes. A Polish Jew, he had been forced out of Warsaw before the beginning of the war and had only lived in the United States for six years before being drafted. Most of his service had been in the Air Force where, for two years, he had stoked furnaces at an officer's club.

Poor Irving. He was bewildered by what had happened to him. I suppose Mac, Green, Crosby and I looked grim and battle-hardened that first night he and the other two replacements first saw us in Strassfeld. We had not shaved for several days and our uniforms were dirty and ragged. We had collected straw and dumped it on the floor of the battered house where we were staying and when the three men came in, we were lying on it talking by the light of a candle we had made by melting wax in a C-ration can.

Under our supervision, the three replacements made up their "big rolls," wrapping all their possessions, except a blanket and a poncho, in their shelter calves. Irving's roll was enormous. He had saved everything he had brought overseas with him, including his gas-proof clothing and a large supply of cigarettes, even though he didn't smoke. It was simply impossible for him to let go of anything.

With our help, he managed to make up a "little roll." But even it was filled with soap, cigarettes, a can of shoe impregnate and other useless items. He packed while asking a series of worried questions. He seemed to fear that a German would pop in at any moment from behind one of the walls and engage him in hand to hand combat. The next morning we found he had stood guard all night without ammunition in his rifle because he was "afraid I might shoot somebody."

Late the following day we loaded aboard trucks and went on eastward across the Rhineland. The country had become hilly again. We passed through regular plots of forest. We found we were driving between the columns of the 60th Regiment. We thought this peculiar. Just as we began to wonder about it the trucks stopped and we heard shells exploding somewhere near the head of the column.

Everyone hung over the edge of the trucks, ready to climb down and seek shelter. Officers milled about in confusion for several minute and then the convoy started up again, moving more rapidly this time. We had come down the wrong road.

We pulled into a large cobblestone farmyard beside

a moated house a few miles farther on, and unloaded.

Soon we were marching again and in a short time we found ourselves in a forest of huge trees, crossed here and there by muddy roads and packed with pile after pile of ammunition of all kinds, boxes of egg grenades, huge 16-inch shells, boxes of rifle and mortar ammunition.

We walked all day through the ammunition depot without meeting anyone except an army movie cameraman. As the day passed, I became increasingly conscious of the load I was carrying. I still had the BAR. I was also packing two blankets, a poncho, several extra bandoleers of ammunition, two grenades, a shovel, my canteen, a BAR ammunition belt, several rations and my helmet.

I was still wearing the overshoes I had been issued at the replacement depot on the way back to the front. They had been soaked with water several times and they made walking difficult. That day they made my feet sore and tender so that night I left my overshoes beside the road.

I was happy when we finally stopped our apparently aimless wandering in a town called Pech. All I can remember of our stop there is that I slept in a bedroom in a large bedstead under a down quilt as if I were dead.

In the morning it was misty and raining again. We were back on a muddy road which led through more trees and hills toward what seemed to be a town. We walked slowly and occasionally we would hear the sound of artillery to the north at Bonn where the First Division was attacking.

The road dipped down into a cut between two steep

banks and ended at a great mound of earth. After we had clambered over its edge, we could see it was a tank trap, a large pit, 12 feet square with walls of logs on either side. It was another useless project of the Volksturm.

Our tanks went to the left and found another road. The infantry remained on the slope of the sunken road. As we walked, we heard the sudden heavy boom of a demolition and saw a bright red flash in the misty, early morning sky. The Germans were blowing up the bridge across the Rhine at Bonn.

Houses appeared at the edge of the road, bigger and finer houses than we had seen so far in Germany. We climbed up out of the roadway and searched a few of them. It was clear we had arrived in a large city and if we attempted to clear it before the day was over, we still would not be able to look in every building.

In one house we found a short, squat *feldwebel*, or rather he ran out and surrendered to us. He told me, in a hoarse, happy voice, that he had been waiting all night for us to appear. He waved a *passerschein* dropped by Allied aircraft which promised him food and a warm place to sleep. Flattery told me to escort him to company headquarters. The little German insisted he and I go back to the house where he had spent the night. There we found his pack stuffed with goodies, blankets, cigars and smoking tobacco.

We had a long walk before we finally found the company command post group. The platoons were being spread more and more widely as they moved through town. I finally was able to drop off my prisoner at a large fancy inn, the exterior decorated with deer antlers.

Then I began my long search back and forth through crowded streets trying to find the second platoon again.

People had begun to appear from everywhere. They clustered in curious knots at street corners, stood in doorways and looked from windows. I found some of the third platoon talking to a priest near a church. They told me the second platoon was farther down the street.

I walked along among the Germans, the only American in sight, smiling as I went. They either looked at me without expression or smiled back. They seemed to be happy.

At one corner a group of people called me over, saying *"Kamerad, kamerad,"* words that we were to hear again and again in the months ahead. I found they were clustered around a young German soldier. He, too, was smiling. The reason was obvious. A long thin-necked wine bottle stuck from the corner of his foodsack. He was quite drunk.

"Hello," I said, for lack of anything else to say.

He said nothing, but with a grand gesture gave me his rifle. I smashed its stock against the curb, unslung my BAR and marched him back to the CP group.

Once again I started on my journey back to the platoon. Finally, I found them crouched along a stone wall on a street lined with large prosperous houses. With them was a group of ten anxious Russians in German uniforms, part of an *Ost* regiment. They, too, had just surrendered and were afraid they were about to be shot.

Back to company headquarters I went, again, with the ten Russians. I was growing weary of all the tramping to and fro over the pavement. By the time I got back to the platoon a third time, they had taken cover in the houses.

Up ahead in a field, according to the Russians, the

Germans had unlimbered a horse drawn artillery battery. Soon it began to fire, its first shells striking in a field to our left.

Later rounds blew roof tiles from a house down the street. We prudently withdrew to the cover of the basement. Sitting there in the half darkness, I was surprised to hear a voice in English say, "I say, is it safe down here?" I turned to see an elderly lady, her husband and son, sitting on a covered sofa looking anxiously out a small window which opened on the street.

"Oh, I guess so," I said, and I began to talk to them.

We soon found out they were German, but had spent many years in England before the war. Now they lived in a suburb of Bad Godesburg, which was the city we were approaching.

Sitting there in the cellar, we had a pleasant, infinitely polite conversation as if war were many miles removed from us. The woman could not understand why the Germans were firing upon their own people. I tried to explain they had done this before in the Rhineland, but she could not grasp this reality.

The boy, their son, looked at me with interest. They explained he was the German equivalent of 4F. He had kidney trouble.

Later our mortars began to fire and the artillery ceased. We went back upstairs where the lady made us all a pot of coffee (somehow I fancied it should have been tea) and then we took our leave, feeling as if we had enjoyed a pleasant social call.

With the artillery battery out of the way, we moved to the end of the street and out across the open field where a dead horses and the overturned guns of the artillery lay, into the main part of Bad Godesburg. Shells were still falling somewhere. We could hear them. But they were no longer close.

We met a man looking sadly at the windows of his hotel. They were large, made of frosted glass, and had all been broken.

"*Fenster kaput*," I said, smiling.

It seemed to amuse him and he said, "*Ja, alles kaput.*"

We walked down the street without bothering to search houses anymore, but still with caution, pressing into doorways and hugging walls. In the center of town we did not find as many people standing about, perhaps because of the artillery fire, but bed sheets and pillowcases had been hung from the windows as tokens of surrender. It was apparent the city was ours without much of a battle.

A few more turns and we came to a place where the buildings were farther apart. There across a flat shelf of land moving muddy and swift between the nearer shore and the high bank beyond we saw, at last, the Rhine.

20

All the fire from the enemy had stopped by the time we reached the river, but we did not go all the way to the shore. A patrol was sent to a boathouse and soon reported back. There were no German soldiers anywhere on the west bank of the river. We entered the houses along the shore to settle down for the night.

The third squad was divided into halves. Each half went to houses on opposite sides of the road to the boathouse. My half knocked on the door of a large gray, stone building. An elderly lady with gray hair answered. I explained, somewhat apologetically, that we planned to spend the night with her.

She seemed confused, but asked us in. After a long discussion we agreed to take over a room on the third floor. Its window faced the house across the road. Mac waved from one of its windows. It was not possible to see the river bank from our room, however. So when night came we stood guard in the living room before a large french window which looked out on a balastraded terrace, the river and the opposite shore.

The whole house reflected wealth. The most impressive item in the building so far as we were concerned, however, was a flush toilet, the first we had seen in months. We used it whenever we could find an opportunity.

The next morning I walked over to Mac's house. It was even grander than ours. The front door was glass, protected by a delicate ironwork design. Inside was a dark wood paneled hall and a beautiful dining room with a great shiny oak table. A deep blue carpet sank luxuriously under my dirty combat books. Mac and his half the squad had slept on the floor in a second story bedroom. They found its carpet a luxury, too.

The woman who lived in the house viewed all of us as intruders, but was particularly outraged at a German shell that exploded in the street outside during the night, breaking the glass front door.

21

Unfortunately our stay in Bad Godesburg came to an end the next day. After dark, we were relieved by the 7th Armored Division. We left the big houses and hiked back through town to what had been a hospital. We slept there briefly and then boarded trucks for an unknown destination.

Rumors had been circulating about a crossing of the Rhine near Cologne. We believed we were heading north to take part in this. We soon lost our sense of direction and could not tell if we were going north or south.

For several hours we seemed to wander about the shouldered banks of the river, losing sight of it now and then. Once we passed through the 99th Division, groups of glum looking men camped in the middle of an open field around smoky fires.

Finally, we dropped down out of the hills toward the river again past a pretty yellow church and reached a small town. Trucks with corps markings on their bumpers stood about the railway station. Everyone was moving with a sense of urgency. We could see the lower part of town near the river had been heavily shelled. Shells were falling somewhere down river, too. We could hear them explode. But no one offered us any explanation of what was happening or where we were.

We dismounted the trucks and in a short time the order to move out came. We started down through town. We went slowly at first, talking to the men standing beside the houses as we moved. From one of them we learned we were in Remagen.

137

As we neared the river, we could see K and I Companies begin to run. This was puzzling for no artillery shells were falling.

The long column of men moved and stopped, moved and stopped until at last we reached the open space by the river.

Then we saw why they had been running. The pavement was pocked with shell holes. Beside the road was a half-track with a dead American in it and beyond that were engineers looking at us from foxholes they had dug in a vineyard.

We dashed across the open space to the Ludendorf Bridge. It stretched intact across the Rhine. A huge sign was nailed to the space between its two nearest round towers. It read, "You Are Crossing the Rhine With Dry Feet Through the Courtesy of the Ninth Armored Division."

Before we could grasp the importance of having a bridge over the river, we were walking across it, looking down through the railroad tracks it carried at the brown water of the river. In a few minutes we were on the other side.

We turned right beneath a high, stony hill, later to be called Flak Hill, and marched down a road along the river bank to the village of Kasbach.

The German side of the river was packed with men, prisoners, and vehicles waiting patiently to cross the river back to Remagen. Now and then a shell would scream across the river and strike either the bridge or the ground near it and someone would be wounded. Multiple 50 caliber machine guns were lined up in the vineyards along the steep slopes of the eastern shore.

That night we slept in Kasbach, crowded together on the first floor of a house. Late the next afternoon we moved to the town of Unkel on the opposite side of the bridgehead. To do so, we had to walk back down the river road beneath the bridge. As we approached it, we could see it was being shelled. Explosions would rocket off its east pier at regular intervals.

As we reached a point just under the bridge, we all ran. I dropped a can of C-rations and stopped to pick it up. Bruner, who was behind me, pushed me on.

"Man, a C-ration ain't worth that much," he said.

Just as he finished speaking, a shell struck the bridge and we all fell flat. Its fragments did not strike near us, however, and we got up and walked on.

In Unkel we were again billeted in a single house. Next morning we moved down the bank of the river still farther to Rheinbreitbach and began to climb the bluffs eastward from the river.

In a short time we were in the woods again. The sun had come out and it was a beautiful day. Below us the Rhine shone in the misty afternoon and except for the distant sound of artillery, it was unlike the war we had known during the past months.

We passed through more piles of ammunition, most of it huge 16 inch shells and powder formed into strips like licorice. Again we seemed to be wandering about and we had the feeling no one seemed to know where we were supposed to be going.

At the top of the bluffs, we turned down a dirt road and were ordered into a ditch. Soon three light tanks drove up, consulted with Captain McClelland and other company and battalion officers. Then they disappeared down the road.

We moved forward into the woods, circling an old, but huge bomb crater until we reached a small clearing. Since we were the reserve company that day, up stream and down engineers were working hard to place pontoon bridges. The one to the north was almost half finished, but that afternoon it was knocked out by a bomb. The engineers had to start construction all over again.

That day the bridgehead was only about four miles long. Parts of the 78th Division, the 9th Armored and our 47th Regiment were holding its perimeter. It was as yet too small for us to be committed to action.

Suddenly everyone and everything seemed close together after the separation of the Rhineland. We felt as the troops must have at Omaha Beach, confined and hurried with the sense that we must break out of the area as soon as we could.

Space was short in Kasbach. The entire second platoon was moved into the first floor of a house. We were told to stay indoors, but it was impossible to get anyone to obey this order. Too much was going on outside.

The day was overcast, but every half hour or so German planes would drop down out of the overcast to try to bomb the bridges. When they did antiaircraft guns for miles around would open fire, filling the air with red tracers. We became infected with the fever and some eager riflemen even fired their pistols and rifles.

Late in the afternoon one plane, a stuka, was shot down as it dove to bomb the bridge. We saw it nose slowly down out of the clouds, drop its bomb and then start to climb again. As it did, the dotted red lines of tracers converged on its dark shape. It burst into a ball of flame and crashed in the hills to the north. We heard later the pilot had parachuted safely.

Toward evening a company of the 99th Division came marching through town. It had crossed the river rapidly as we had and its men were panting as they climbed the hill beside our house in the rain. We stood at the gate. The men in the 99th had not shaved for several days. They had thrown ponchos over their packs and now looked like human camels. "Where you guys been?" someone asked, joking.

We sat under trees to wait while K and I Companies tried to force their way down the road through the trees to a village beyond the woods. They did not have much success. The attached tanks would not move forward unless the infantry went first. The infantry company commanders wanted the tanks to go first. It was an argument through all the war and one which had to be settled a different way each time it arose.

We sat in the shadows of the trees for a long time, smoking, talking, and making feeble efforts at digging foxholes. At last the battalion commander asked our company to send out a patrol around the flank of one of the lead companies. Marshall was picked as patrol leader. He had made most of the patrols for the platoon since he had come back from the battalion patrol.

After about an hour he came back with one of his men wounded. A bullet had creased the man's back. The squad had followed a stream bed for a long way. Marshall said he kept hearing German voices, and said, "I just kept by-passing them."

One he could not by-pass. It was a German machine gun outpost. That was where his man had been wounded. As soon as they were fired on, the patrol melted back to an assembly area and bandaged the wounded man. Then they returned to where we were waiting.

The battalion commander and regimental commander were so pleased with the patrol they told Marshall they would recommend him for a battlefield commission.

In the meantime, we had all been ordered to get our gear and follow the path that Marshall had explored. It was quite dark by the time we reached the streambed. But we kept going forward. Once planes, apparently German, flew over and the antiaircraft by the bridge opened up, filling the air with shrapnel. Some of it fell near us in spent pieces.

Soon it was night. It became increasingly difficult to keep contact with one another in the darkness. The stream bed meandered back and forth. It grew deeper and narrower, but there was little water in it. We came to a place where the stream branched into two forks, both of them too narrow to walk in. We had to climb to level land and walk through the woods.

We had only moved about fifty feet into the trees when a concentration of artillery shells burst all about us. The first one struck a tree almost overhead, showering its fragments down on our heads. A great red glare bloomed in the woods and dirt showered on us from another explosion not far away. I turned and sprinted back to the cover of the streambed, followed by the rest of the squad and eventually the rest of the company. Chaos followed for a few moments, with squads and platoons mixed together.

Wagner and Kalman had been wounded, Kalman in the hand slightly and Wagner by a hot piece of metal that stuck him between his BAR belt and his skin. Ten or eleven other men had been hurt, most of them in the first platoon and in several heavy machine gun squads from M Company that had been attached to us earlier.

In spite of the confusion, I felt very collected. I bandaged a wounded man's head and told him to follow the creek bed back to the aid station. Then I saw Irving sitting high on the creek bank, peering out over the edge through his thick glasses.

"What the hell are you doing?" I asked.

"I'm getting into a firing position," he said.

"Get down here," I shouted back. "No one's going to fire at you with a rifle."

Although we never knew for sure, we always believed the shells had been directed into the woods by the 78th Division in the mistaken belief that we were Germans passing in front of their lines.

It soon developed that the wounded could not be sent back down the streambed to the aid station because it was moving and would rejoin us later. We were not sure where. This meant we had to take the wounded with us.

We were headed toward a village called Kalenborn which was across an open field, around the corner of the woods. More disorganized than organized, we began to cross the field in the dark. I carried Pancho, the same Mexican-American sergeant who had greeted us in Ginnick. Pancho had been wounded in the foot, couldn't walk and was very heavy. After I had carried him for awhile he had to stop and vomit. Then he started to crawl on his hands and knees. Someone else picked him up and we took turns carrying him into town.

Just as we reached the outskirts of Kalenborn a stream of red tracers went off over our heads—obviously American, since German tracers were white. But we managed to reach its first buildings and deposit the wounded without difficulty.

22

We spent the night in a large three-storied house across the road from where we had taken the wounded. It once had had wide windows across the side that faced the street, but they had all been blown out by shellfire. It was like sleeping on a raised open railway platform.

The next morning we woke to find the wounded had been evacuated to the south through the 78th Division lines. We had met some of their troops coming from that direction in Kalenborn, a town set on a ridge that sloped gently into a valley. West of the town was a railroad embankment and an underpass that opened to the street.

When it was light a German tank, one of four that had been holding up the advance of K and I Companies, started its engine just on the other side of the underpass. We could see blue smoke rise from its engine and hear it ticking over softly. Hurriedly, Flattery got the platoon's two trembling bazooka men out on the porch, ready should the tank come down the street.

Like all infantrymen, I had a great terror of tanks. I went to the back of the house and checked to see how far away the woods lay. For almost an hour we hung suspended on a wire of tension, waiting for something to happen. Finally, the tank's engine began to roar and it moved away from the underpass, using the protection of the railway embankment until it disappeared. A short time later K and I Companies emerged from the woods and linked up with us.

Later in the afternoon 78th Division troops moved in front of us, pinching us off from the front line.

That evening I came out on the front porch of the house to find Irving reading his pocket prayer book and looking at a picture of a woman.

"Who's that?" I said.

"It's my wife," he said. "I'm taking a last look at her before I die."

That evening Marshall's squad was again sent on patrol. This time they were to go to the lower part of Kalenborn, Unterkalenborn, to check for enemy. The orders were as ambiguous as usual, "Go down and have a look. If there isn't anything there, the rest of the company will come down. If there is, come back."

Shortly after dark (and their departure) the company received a radio request from Marshall for someone to pick up two prisoners he had captured. Mac, Green and I volunteered to carry out the duty. We stumbled down the littered street through the lines of the 78th Division, just sitting down to eat, toward the dark houses below. On a hill to the left a tank, probably one of those we had heard at the railway embankment had been hit by artillery shells and was burning. Its ammunition caught fire. Every now and then a shell would explode, sending bright yellow balls of flame into the air. It looked like a Roman candle.

By its light, we reached the first house at the edge of Unterkalenborn to find Marshall, his squad and the two prisoners in the basement. From the prisoners Marshall had discovered there was an entire German company in the village.

The prisoners, had been sent to the house as an outpost and had walked into the patrol's arms. They were not happy at being captured, an exception to the usual rule, and Marshall wanted to get them to the rear as soon as possible.

We had just prepared to return with the prisoners when we heard German voices on the road below. Under the circumstances, the best thing seemed to be to beat a retreat. We all climbed out a basement window and hurried back up the road, tangling ourselves in a "daisy chain" of antitank mines the 78th Division had set out as we did. Fortunately, we were not heavy enough to set them off.

The 78th men were still eating as we passed through their lines and we managed to steal cake from their meal as we moved to the rear.

After Marshall's report of the patrol, "heavy harassing fire" was laid on the town for the rest of the night. By morning the village was badly damaged.

At dawn we took up the attack again, again passing through the 78th and dodging in and out of the long line of houses that descended the hill. In one house an old woman who was either insane or stubborn. Despite my orders to her in German to remain where she was, she walked off down the street in the direction of the enemy.

We reached the village school house at the bottom of the hill. It had been all but destroyed by artillery fire. The lower windows had been blown out, the roof had caved in and two of the walls on the upper story had fallen off. We stopped in the school room. Through one of the big windows, Bruner saw a German soldier running across a field to the east. Bruner shot and killed him. He died slowly. We heard his cry of "Kamerad, hilfe,hilfe, hilfe," until it finally trailed away into silence.

Most of the inhabitants of the village had assembled

in the basement of the school house. As soon as we arrived, they wanted to get out to return to their homes. We had considerable difficulty in keeping them in the shelter. From our shelter, we could see Germans on the hill opposite now and then. Madeley, the first sergeant, who had replaced Sgt. Ogborne, came down to take a look. He borrowed my BAR and with Dumas spotting for him with a pair of glasses, began firing at a wall near a building on the opposite hill.

The fire was returned immediately. A mortar round burst on top of the school house. Plaster and dirt rained down on us. When it had stopped, I looked around to find I was alone in the room, everyone else had taken shelter at the bottom of the cellar steps. I soon joined them. Madeley made a hurried departure to the rear.

By afternoon the Germans had moved to the east and we could walk about the village without danger. The villagers were allowed to go back to their badly damaged houses and found they had been looted by German soldiers.

The third squad climbed to the second floor of the school house over stairs which had almost disappeared. There we blacked out the windows and made beds on the floor. We had just settled down for the night when a tank destroyer parked outside fired a single round which knocked down all the blackout blinds and forced us to put out our lights. We went to bed in the dark.

23

We remained in Unterkalenborn all next morning while other rifle companies moved ahead of us. The bridgehead had now been expanded sufficiently to put the bridge out of German artillery range and armor had begun to cross the river for a breakout to the east, into open country. Although we did not know it at the time, only a thin crust of German troops lay between us and undefended country.

That afternoon we walked down the valley through a narrow pass in the hills to Hollerbach, held by the Second Battalion. It was an easy sunshiny stroll until we reached the first house in town. Then a tank, somewhere in the hills ahead, opened fire. But its shells exploded harmlessly on the road.

The Germans apparently had observation, however. Soon shells struck the village and then marched up over the hill to our right in an orderly fashion as they adjusted their fire. The spent fragments from the nearest explosions fell on our backs. It was frightening, but interesting. Yet it also was clear we could not remain where we were for long.

The men at the head of the column leapt to their feet and dashed across the short space to the first house in the village. Then we began moving from house to house. It was a small town and because the Second Battalion was already there, it was a short while before we could find a place to take cover. Finally, the third squad came to rest in a little house at the edge of the village. It was built of cement blocks. A shell had exploded not far from one of its walls, pocking and piercing it in many places.

A young couple had built it. Apparently, it was their first home. The wife, a small, blackhaired, but not pretty girl came after awhile to get something from the cellar. She had been crying. Most of her valuables had been stored there, silver, glassware, blankets and clothes. But the Second Battalion had looted the upstairs and piles of dirty junk lay on the floor covered with crumbled gray rubble from the broken walls.

One of the men from the Second Battalion put his arm around her shoulders as she came in.

"Hi,ya, baby," he said grinning.

"Bitte," she said, looking at him and seeking compassion, but without struggling against the arm.

"She's a good gal," the soldier said. "We had a lot of fun last night."

I never knew whether he had really raped her or not. I tried to talk to her, but she only wanted to be left alone. We asked if she would cook us some potatoes. She did, boiling them in a pan and serving them with liquor she said was schnapps. As we ate, she begged us not to wreck anything further in the house. We did nothing but eat and then went outside and slumped against the wall of the house in the sun.

Late in the afternoon we moved on. Again we were the reserve platoon. Shells had been falling infrequently about the village. We could hear firing in the hills beyond it, but we were able to move about without difficulty. We threaded our way down the town's single street and climbed across the fields into the hills that rose beyond the sides of a little valley.

Woods crowned the slopes, the sun shone and flickered through the trees. The company was strung out in a long single line and moved like a snake in loose coils among the trees. Now and then it stopped. Sometimes there would be a brief flurry of running, then the pace would slacken and we would halt. We heard several shells shriek into the trees ahead of us and soon a litter team passed, sweating as they carried a wounded man. A short time later and they were back again, this time with a blanketed figure which bumped and rolled on the litter. It was a man from the first platoon.

As the light began to fade, we halted at the bottom of a hollow and saw Captain NcClelland and the company command post group come over its edge. McClelland walked with a jaunty step and cracked a joke as he saw us. We all smiled.

The draw seemed to be as far as we were going for the night. Everyone lay down in its shallow curve and began loosening their equipment. K Company passed, moving to our right flank through the woods. Captain Dickie, the K Company commander, and Captain McClelland exchanged a few unkind remarks with one another in a friendly way.

Then it grew dark and we learned, in the devious fashion that soldiers always do, that the first and third platoons had advanced to a ridge a short distance ahead, only to be met with rifle fire. They had stopped there and were waiting for some kind of maneuver by someone, no one knew who.

I had begun to feel ill, one of the few times I did not feel well during combat. I concluded it was the schnapps I had drunk earlier in the day.

As I lay there, I heard Flattery talk to Captain McCelland and then to Mac. The third squad was ordered to its feet. We were going on a patrol. We were to follow K Company's path through the woods until we found its command post. There we were to ask Captain Dickie if his flank touched the Cologne-Frankfurt auto-bahn. When we had this information, we were to go to the flank, cross the highway and enter a village called Birken. After that, we were to follow the standing or-der: "If there's anybody there, come back and tell us and we'll bring the company up. If there's nothing, just come back and tell us."

We started off, climbing slowly through the woods. After a few hundred yards we came to a great open plowed field. From it we could see the white beams of artificial moonlight from searchlights set up at the Remagen bridge. The field was ringed with the dark shapes of woods as far as we could see.

Feeling naked and exposed, we walked carefully to the middle of the open circle of ground and looked about. K Company was nowhere in site. We listened. We could hear nothing.

We started toward the crest of land, but we still couldn't find K Company. I had begun to feel sicker and Wagner had begun to cough hollowly. Each time he did, we hissed at him to be quiet, but he kept hacking away. When he tried to stifle the cough, he choked and made even more noise.

We stopped uncertainly by some low bushes, won-dering what we should do. Miserable as I was, I could stand it no longer.

"Wait a minute," I said. I walked away from the rest of the squad toward the trees. It was, in retrospect, a stupid thing to do, but I felt so sick I no longer cared. At the edge of the woods, I trod carefully on fallen leaves.

Carl F. Heintze

After my eyes became accustomed to the dimmer light, I saw two shapes on the round which were unmistakably human. Near them I could see two rifles leaning against a tree. Cautiously, I stepped over to feel the shape of the helmets. One of them suddenly came alive and said, "What ya want?"

"I'm from L Company," I said. "We're looking for the CP."

"Oh. It's down the road," the soldier said, vaguely.

"Okay," I said. "Don't shoot when I bring the rest of them back."

He mumbled something and went back to sleep.

I gathered the rest of the patrol from the field. We picked our way past the two sleeping men and started down the dirt road through the woods, waiting for someone to challenge us. No one did. We walked on, making as much noise as we dared, but without seeing anyone.

After we had gone about a hundred yards, we stopped, perplexed. I was sick and angry. I sat down. Just as I did, there was a bright flash, explosions and shots popped over our heads.

We had walked through the entire K Company perimeter and were now on the opposite enemy side of the company. We had walked past two new replacements without being challenged. They took us for Germans. One had thrown a white phosphorous grenade, fortunately in the wrong direction. The other had fired his BAR, but because we were on the downward slope of the hill, all the shots went wide.

After what seemed like several minutes, but which

was probably a much shorter time, we managed to yell above the firing that we were Americans. The firing stopped. We walked back up the hill, got new directions and finally found the CP, a group of black lumps under a tree. It was Captain Dickie and his runners covered with blankets.

Dickie told us he did not know where the autobahn was. He had been unable to find it and had stopped for the night before he reached the height of land. This, so far as we were concerned, finished off the patrol. We went back across the field, found the L Company command post and reported what we had found.

But we were ordered to make another try for the highway and the village.

The second patrol left Wagner behind and picked up several other men. I had begun to feel really sick by this time, but I went along anyway. We retraced our path through the woods to the field. This time I took the lead. I was sure the highway lay along the crest of the hill, but strangely enough we could not see it.

I moved back and forth over the plowed field, looking and looking until I was not sure what I was seeing. Then I looked down. There, to my surprise, was the highway. It ran through a cut in the ridge. That was why we had been unable to see it. I slithered down the side of the highway near an overpass and dashed across the cement to the other side. Sick and tired, I climbed upward, moving toward the shape of houses I could just see above the farther bank.

I emerged directly in front of a German foxhole. Luckily, it was empty.

I looked back to see if the others were following me

and then walked to the first house. The artificial moonlight reflected off its white wall. A great hole had been made in the wall by a shell. The houses beyond were sunk in shadow. I stood for a moment looking and as I did, I heard the stamp of feet directly in front of me. I was certain it was a German sentry, stamping his feet to keep them warm. In a panic I turned and jumped back over the highway cut to join the others.

"What's the matter?" Mac said.

"There's somebody up there," I said.

"Where?"

I pointed. Everyone looked. It was a horse, loose from his barn. Sick as I was, I had been mistaken.

After that I do not remember much. We searched the houses, found them empty and made the long climb back down the hill to the rest of the company. As soon as we returned to the village, I found a bed in a second story room and fell into it beside Wagner, just as dawn was breaking. I slept most of the day, but now and then I would wake to find Wagner coughing in my face. The next day I had the cough. It was many weeks before it was completely gone. I did not drink any more schnapps.

24

We stayed in Birken for five days during which the sun shone, the days warmed and the armor continued to roll across the bridges to build up behind our lines around the perimeter of the bridgehead. No shells fell upon Birken, although I and K Companies, in villages further eastward, were shelled regularly each day.

Why we remained immune, I never knew for Birken was on a height of land next to the highway. From it we could see for miles, in every direction. An artillery observer moved into the attic of the house we occupied and we spent the afternoons with him watching as he called for concentrations (targets).

At night the rifle platoons took turns outposting the village in the woods that lay below it. It was a small village, only five houses, and there were few places to sleep indoors.

The breakout from the bridgehead began on the fifth night. L and I Companies moved abreast across the hills to the southeast, down a deep valley and up a hill beyond. There they separated, each attacking a different village.

An hour after dark we moved out in a long single file into the valley. Soon the word came back down the line, "Watch it on the right." Then, "Watch it on the left." And finally, "Watch it behind you." This last was probably a joke.

We struggled downhill through thick pine forest, forded a shallow stream and then climbed the other side, crashing and stumbling in the heavy undergrowth. A red German rocket exploded in the night far above us and the white of German machine gun tracers sailed out over the valley, but the enemy did not seem to know where we were.

In the darkness the column coiled and looped in confusion. Finally, it broke into a clearing just below the village which was our objective. Only an undefended Volksturm log blockhouse stood in the way. The village was empty.

It was growing light by the time we had searched its houses. We did not stop, but moved on to a second town, Oberplag. The forest had disappeared. We followed a dirt road up over a bare hill. As soon as the entire company was spread along the road, a machine gun began to fire over our heads. Everyone took shelter in a shallow drainage ditch beside the road.

Tired and sleepy, we lay there for a few minutes and then tried to move forward. The machine gun fired again. We went back to the ditch. Captain McClelland, who had found a bomb crater up the road for shelter, called for smoke shells to be fired ahead of the company. We tried to move again. The machine gun fired again.

No one was wounded, but no one wanted to move. The company commander asked for tank support, but the tanks were all with I Company which had run into more serious trouble in the second village. So we lay on our bellies in the ditch and talked and smoked. The sun was warm and it was not unpleasant. In a little while I fell asleep. When I awoke, it was afternoon. I urinated beneath me in the ditch and then crawled a few feet forward until my helmet touched Wagner's boots. He was writing a poem to his wife. It was her birthday.

At last, just as dusk was approaching, a tank and a tank destroyer rolled up the road. We got to our feet and walked into Oberplag. Two or three houses were smoking and wrecked from artillery fire, but the Germans had fled. People came out of their cellars and just as it got dark one of our attached heavy machine guns set up on the edge of the village and fired across the valley at a single retreating enemy soldier. He dodged and weaved among the red tracers and disappeared over the hilltop without being hit.

That night the Third Armored Division struck out from the bridgehead, moving many miles with only scattered opposition. In the morning we loaded into trucks, crossed the Wied River below the tumbled arches of a blown autobahn bridge and followed the path left by the tanks.

By early afternoon we had reached our objective, a town whose name I have forgotten. We climbed down from the trucks and lay down in the street against the side of a house and went to sleep. In a few minutes, however, our kitchen trucks appeared and a convoy of trucks, tanks and tank destroyers was formed. We loaded aboard and set out again.

All the rest of that day and into the night we rode eastward, passing through village after village, through woods, past rag-tag groups of prisoners and displaced persons, past curious Germans lining the streets of their towns until finally we stopped for the night at another village.

The breakthrough, the long haul up through the Westerwald around the edge of the Ruhr had begun. We had reached the crest of the wave of victory and rode on it, moving forward to the point where it would crash on a further shore, the Elbe. The months of winter, of woods and darkness, of patient, but costly attack, consolidate and attack, even the goal of the Rhine were behind. We now knew with certainty the war would soon be over. Only the question of which day, which hour remained.

And as we moved, we were a part of power, of strength which had been slow to form, but whose determination and certainty had never been in doubt to us. For that single short week moving, always moving forward, we were that vaunted and often mentioned crusade. On every road we could see was the real proof of our authority, trucks, tanks, jeeps, ambulances, tank destroyers, vans, guns and men.

Before us each town and village spread its sheets and pillow cases as a signal of surrender. We were a tidal wave of power, we were the conquerors. There would never be a time quite like it again.

And yet it was all a great blur, as we drove mile after mile without hearing a shot or seeing the explosion of a shell. Towns were only names on road signs. We saw them and forgot them.

Where once we had known a single hill for days or weeks, now they passed in a few moments. We went down roads without roadblocks. We met enemy tanks, but they were burned and abandoned. It seemed nothing could stand in our way.

What do I remember of those five days?

I remember Diensbach and the old man in whose house we stayed who had smoked tea because his tobacco was gone. We gave him a can of Prince Albert and he cried.

I remember the man somewhere beside the road

who stretched his hand toward ours and shouted insanely, "*Ich bin Social Democrat.*"

I remember the flour mill and the barn where we slept high in a hay loft as soft as a feather bed.

I remember the view from one hill of a valley with three roads running through it, each one lined bumper to bumper with vehicles of all kinds moving to the northeast.

I remember the endless signs on telephone poles saying "Timber-wolf Up," and bearing the patch of the 104th Division.

I remember Crosby saying over and over, "It's going to end on Easter Sunday," and I remember the dusty trucks of the Third Armored Division loaded with prisoners, the bare green hills, the woods, the villages and towns, the endless swaying motion of the trucks, the hard seats, the happy faces of the platoon.

Most of all I remember the emotion of it all: a feeling of youth, of victory, of the departure from death, motion, speed, power, the knowledge that together we were this vast thing and singly we had each helped to build it.

And yet it was not the end. What we had longed for, victory, and what we had expected, peace, were still not to be ours. Before we would see them, we would suffer again and fight and be wounded and die.

25

We had been riding all day, coming each evening to some new place in the deep valleys of the Westerwald. We were tired of riding and we leaned against one another, sometimes falling asleep for a moment or two, then waking with a start, only to fall asleep again. We never seemed to get enough sleep, no matter how long we stopped in any one place. I suppose we averaged about five hours a night, but our weariness had a cumulative quality. It was like a burden whose weight was sometimes temporarily lifted, but from which we were never completely free.

The truck ground up over the crest of a hill, coasted a few hundred yards down the road and stopped. The end of motion woke the sleeping and brought the waked to attention. We stood up to look across a wide valley whose far end was lined with green fields, deepening into black in the twilight. Beneath us was a town, almost hidden under the slope of the hill. Only a church steeple was visible.

"Wasn't that artillery?" someone said.

We all listened. It was a sound we dreaded and one we had almost become unfamiliar with.

"You're hearing things," someone else said, but just then we all heard the deep rumble-bumps of a gun in the town below. It was artillery.

Glumly we all sat down and waited as the trucks jerked and stopped, jerked and stopped to the bottom of the valley and turned into the town. By the time we had reached the first buildings, it was dark. We unloaded in the darkness, not knowing where we were or what we were to do. We stood in resignation by the tailgate of the truck, until finally Flattery came up with orders.

The third squad was separated from the rest of the platoon and guided to one of the battalion's anti-tank guns. We climbed aboard its half-track and rode through the dark streets to the far edge of town. There in a small house, we made ready to sleep while the gun crew set their piece up in position to guard the road.

Word had been passed around that a tank attack was expected next morning. We were to provide infantry support for the anti-tank gun. It was my first assignment as squad leader, a position to which I had risen because of the departure of Bill Shaw, the platoon guide, on a Paris pass. Mac had taken over as platoon guide in his absence. Marshall, a new sergeant named Clow and I were now squad leaders.

I took my men upstairs to the attic, really a hayloft, and we spread our blankets on some straw. But we had hardly arranged for guard reliefs when a jeep drove up and we were ordered to return to the rest of the company. Wearily, we loaded back aboard the anti-tank halftrack and drove back to town. As we did, a German shell screamed in over the rooftops and exploded in a field beyond the town.

The rest of the company was assembled in the street. As we joined them, the company column moved out down the road two abreast. It was a dark night without stars. The high hills covered with pines soared toward the sky on either side of us. The only visible thing was the road before us, curling like a stream of silent white water between the mountains. We stumbled along in a sleepy daze, walking and stopping, walking and

161

stopping as the scouts ahead moved and halted, trying to see.

How long we walked, I do not know. But it must have been several hours. There was no talking, only the sound of our boots on the pavement and the wind in the trees.

Once we passed two men crouched in a ditch. They were from the First Division, but how they came to be there, we never learned.

As dawn broke we stopped and sat on the edge of the road, waiting for someone to tell us what to do. A hill jutted across the sky in front of us and hid the rest of the valley, but we knew that somewhere ahead there was a town. There was always a town somewhere ahead.

Then three tanks and three tank destroyers rumbled up and halted and we were ordered aboard them.

"We're going into town," Flattery yelled at everyone. "Shoot at all the windows."

No one knew exactly what this meant, but we scrambled aboard the tanks purposefully. I, overcome with my importance as a squad leader, sat down next to the gun barrel of the tank I had boarded and stared grimly ahead at the road in the half-gray dawn light.

There were more shouts and suggestions and then the lead tank moved forward with a lurch. In a moment, we were moving, too. We turned around the hill that had blocked our view and saw the highway curled along the high bank of a bill. Then it made another sharp turn under a cliff and disappeared.

By the time we reached the cliff, the lead tank was about to exit from the valley. It had just started to make the turn when there was a flash, a roar. Utter confusion descended on the company.

Everyone fought to get off the tanks and tank destroyers for cover. I raised my rifle, stood up beside the cannon barrel and fired off a clip in the direction of the flash. Another shell ripped over my head, cracking and splintering a tree beside the road. Hurriedly, I jumped to the pavement to look for shelter.

The tank began to back up. Its treads humped over the fallen branch of the tree. The limb skittered across the road toward me and I ran to the other side of the pavement to get out of the way. Someone yelled at the tank commander to stop, but he ignored the order and continued to back up the tank.

Most of the second platoon collected under the cliff. No one had been injured, but we were all frightened and confused. The cliff rose almost vertically above us for twenty feet. Beyond it lay the steep slope of the mountain. On the other side of the road a bank dropped into a little stream and a railroad track, from there was a flat meadow and more steep hills.

We were ringed with hills with almost no room to maneuver. The tanks and tank destroyers could only move on the road (backward, as it turned out) and we knew nothing of what lay in the hills on either side of us. It was, in fact, a perfect place for an ambush, which is why the Germans had picked it to set up a roadblock.

For a few minutes we sat and waited for something to happen or for someone to tell us what to do. Then K Company crossed the road behind us and despite several bursts of machine gun fire disappeared into the hills across the valley. Two litter teams passed on their way to the lead tank. Before long they were back with two wounded.

The lead tank had been struck by an armor-piercing anti-tank shell. The shell, solid metal, had not exploded, but had bounced upward from the bow of the tank, scooping a trough in the metal and wounding the first platoon aid man and two other men. They had all been hit in the feet or legs.

Captain McClelland had been on the second tank. After the shell struck, he and the first platoon had climbed up the steep hillside above the cliff. There they had built up a thin line and tried to locate the Germans.

Without further orders the two remaining tanks and the three tank destroyers stopped in line on the road. We slumped beside the road and looked at them. Time passed. Once or twice we heard firing ahead. Then litter teams went past again, to return with Captain McClelland's radio operator and the first platoon sergeant. Both had been wounded by machine gun bullets.

We looked at them numbly and someone recalled that L Company had always run into trouble on the first day of the month—October 1 in the Huertgen Forest, January 1 on the hill near Elsenborn where I had been wounded and March 1 at Ginnick. Today was April 1.

And then, in the mysterious way in which news travels in the army, we knew that Captain McClelland was dead. I cannot remember anyone telling me it had happened, we just seemed to know. He had been killed by the same burst of fire that had wounded his radioman and the first platoon sergeant.

They had been peeking over the top of a ridge, trying to spot the anti-tank gun. The burst had wounded the radioman in the arm and nicked McClelland. Instead of moving to a new position, he had eased up for another look and had been struck in the face, dying instantly.

So died a fine officer and a good man.

Lt. Ross, his head bent over and his map case stuck determinedly under his arm, passed, going up to take command of the company.

Our trial under the cliff had not ended. An hour later, the Germans moved their gun so they could sight it down the road. They then set the lead tank afire, knocked out the second tank behind it and forced the third tank and the three tank destroyers to back up to the far side of the valley.

The fire created another brief panic. Everyone in the second platoon climbed above the cliff to the woods, where they should have been all the time. There we sat among the trees until late afternoon. Then, as it was growing dark, we started toward the ridge above us in an attempt to outflank the town.

Marshall's squad was in the lead. They emerged from the cover of the woods and began to cross a slanted clearing in the trees. A machine gun fired again, pinning them to the ground.

We circled helplessly around the edge of the clearing trying to find some way to free them from the fire, but we were unable to see them because of rocks above us. Every time they tried to crawl back toward us, the machine gun fired.

Marshall lay behind a small tree and shouted down to us. As he did, he turned his head and opened his mouth and was struck by two bullets. The first went through his open mouth without touching his lips, knocking out two teeth, and emerging from his cheek. That bullet fractured his jawbone. The second passed through the fleshy part of his leg without striking bone.

Flattery tried to build up a firing line to free the squad. But we had no idea where the machine gun was. We crawled up the hillside just as darkness came. In the meantime the German machine gun squad had disappeared.

Everyone came down from the clearing and the litter bearers picked up the wounded. I tried, without success, to find Marshall, to say goodbye.

The platoon reassembled in the darkness and moved back down the hill to the road. The German roadblock had disappeared, too, and so we started forward toward the town, Zuschen, again. But instead of following the road, we were led to scrub brush and formed into a skirmish line. It was a futile maneuver.

The night was so black we could see nothing and we were soon thrashing about in the darkness, in confusion. Lines of men were intersecting with one another. Wagner kept saying over and over again in a litany, "I can't see. I can't see."

Finally, in a kind of lock step we came to a place and heard Lt. Wheel's voice somewhere below us. One by one we dropped down a bank to the road below. From there we walked into town and found the first few houses empty and abandoned.

The entire second platoon crowded into a huge double house, more to see light again than for any other reason, and ate their supper. When we had finished I took two men to search the other half of the house— something we should have done much earlier. We felt our way around the wall of the building and into a kind of cement runway, looking for a door. I had just reached out to grasp the knob when a voice directly in front of me said, in German, "*Kamerad, nicht schiessen.*"

I flipped up my rifle and backed away, saying, "*Raus.*" Two German tankers walked out with their hands in the air. Green shook them down and found a pistol on one of them. We quickly searched the rest of the house, but found it empty.

After we returned with the prisoners, Flattery ordered my squad to move down the street, searching the houses along the way. We had gone only a block or two when we met men from K Company. They had come into town from the hills and had cut across in front of us. Villegas, one of the men from the battalion patrol tthat we had both belonged to, was with them. He told us prisoners believed there were "many SS" still in town. In spite of this, we moved on, searching several more houses before returning to the platoon, but finding nothing.

When we came to what seemed to be the last building, we quit. By this time it was dawn. As it grew light, however, we discovered that the "last" house was only the beginning of Zuschen. It stretched for more than two miles down the valley. We began a renewed search, but it soon became obvious that the Germans had left.

At the far end of town we found a large inn and I moved my squad into it. Most of the windows had been broken by shellfire but I found an upstairs back bedroom with windows intact. Inside was a bed, a wash basin with running water and a dresser. I took off my shoes, pulled a down comforter over me and fell asleep. I had not slept for forty-eight hours.

26

Four hours later Pelky, the platoon runner, shook me awake. It was afternoon, a cloudy afternoon.

"Come on, we're moving out," he said. "Get your squad together."

"Moving out?" I said. "We just got here."

"Yeah, I know, but the 60th got into some kind of trouble. We have to help them out."

Wearily, I got to my feet, found my equipment and rounded up my men from various rooms of the inn. The rest of the platoon was waiting when we arrived on the street. Trucks had appeared from somewhere. We boarded them and rode a short way up the road. The sky was gray and dark and I was in a mood to match it. Marshall was gone, Captain McClelland was dead and I was tired and sleepy.

After a few miles we stopped in a hilltop village that looked down on several deep valleys. Several buildings in the center of the village were still burning.

We found a forlorn group of officers from the 60th Regiment standing beside the road. They were downcast because one of their regiment's battalions had been overrun in the next town. The battalion had captured or occupied the town the night before. Apparently everyone, including their guards, had fallen asleep. A German armored unit, the same one that had attacked us outside Zuschen, had filtered into town and surprised the entire battalion. Even a one in the battalion had been captured.

We had been called forward to cut across the hills from one side, while another company attacked from the opposite direction. We hoped to recapture as many men as we could.

As soon as we were off the trucks and lined up along the roadway we moved out. We plunged down into the valley along the curve of the hill. Across the valley on a high ridge, we could see men moving about. We thought these men were K Company, but later I concluded they were Germans. None of our officers looked through their glasses.

After dipping into the valley, the road began to climb toward the village. It was hard going and we stopped for a rest after a time. As we did, the battalion intelligence officer (who had replaced Lt. Sadler a few days before) came struggling up to the rear of the column.

"Where's Lt. Ross?" he said, gasping for breath.

"Up front," we told him.

"Oh God," he said, as he struggled onward.

Apparently Lt. Ross had read his map incorrectly and we were on the wrong road. It was a fortunate mistake if the village we had seen was occupied by German, not American troops. The young officer did not return and we proceeded up the road.

As we approached the village we ran across an open field and into a large shed. It was filled with abandoned American helmets. We spread out into town and soon discovered it was empty. The Germans had fled.

All the captured men were eventually recovered. By this time the Ruhr pocket had been sealed, but that night we made very sure our guards were up and awake.

27

We struck out again the next morning. As soon as it was light we moving out of the village into the woods beyond. A misty rain began to fall. We were high enough in the Westerwald that patches of snow still lay beneath the pine trees. We no longer had overshoes so our feet were soon wet and cold.

The attack moved down both sides of a highway, along the tops of the mountains toward the town of Winterberg. I Company too the lead at the right and left sides of the road. We moved along I Company's left flank. K Company brought up the rear as a reserve. The woods were patchy, but thick. We crashed through them, passing a huge inn, smaller houses and then came out into a plowed field.

As we moved along, we could see we were on the crest of the range, a long, narrow ridge that disappeared in the misty rain. On its left side there was only a blank gray fog. The natural tendency to follow ground that was as level as possible gradually pulled us away from the road and we lost contact with I Company's left flank. We could only hear their vague shouts through the misty rain.

At last the company stopped and I was delegated to take four men and go back to the big inn we had passed, to find out what had happened.

We started out but soon became lost. I followed our tracks, crossing fields and woods, but it was only after a long search that I finally found the inn. I walked into the front door only to be met with a scene of wild confusion.

A German armored car had just raced down the

highway between the startled ranks of I Company. At the bend of the highway below the house it had come face to face with an American tank destroyer. Although the tank destroyer mounted a 90 millimeter cannon which could have easily blown the half-track off the road, the crews of both vehicles were so startled, they simply looked at each other and then backed away.

All the riflemen in I Company immediately began firing wildly at the half-track. None of them hit it. As I entered the door, Capt. Croonquist, the I Company commander, was frantically shouting over his radio, trying to find his left platoon — the one which should have been in contact with us. Lt. Wheels, our company executive officer, also was there and added to the confusion by dashing back and forth with shouting erratic advice to Capt. Croonquist and my squad.

Just then the platoon sergeant and the missing I Company platoon from its left flank walked in the door. They had heard the shots and had returned to the inn to find out what was happening. This meant there was nothing between the Germans and the inn except trees.

Capt. Croonquist angrily ordered them back to where they were supposed to be. Lt. Wheels sent me back to the second platoon.

When we arrived back at the ridge I found that Clow, the only remaining squad leader except myself, had been wounded. Flattery had gone down the ridge to find the company command post. Mac was in charge. Together he and I set out in the fog which now had replaced the rain in search of the CP. We found it in one of two small summer houses perched on a fold in the ridge. Lt. Ross and his CP group had taken refuge there.

Ross and some of the men were warming themselves

around a stove. The rest were standing outside in the cold, waiting for someone to tell them what to do. No one seemed to have a clear idea what this should be.

Mac went into the room with the CP group and Flattery. I walked into the other bedroom and found the platoon runners and the platoon medic lying on a bed.

I had just started to tell them what had happened at the inn when we heard a bang, crash, Crash, CRASH! A concentration of mortar shells exploded all around the house. As if by magic I saw a fuzz of splinters appear in the wooden wall. The grenade strapped to Pelky, the platoon runner's chest harness parted, spilling red gunpowder on his chest and the medic clutched his leg.

Outside someone cried in pain, "Help me, help me, Jesus Christ, help me."

Flattery rushed out of the next room, grabbed the radio telephone from the radio operator and began shouting at the heavy mortars of N Company to cease firing.

We scrambled to the floor and then got up as we realized the barrage was over — for the time being, at least. Two men dragged the man who had been shouting for help inside the tiny hallway between the two rooms. His chin had been sheared off, one of his legs had been almost cut off, his arm was broken and he had been struck in many other places by bits of shrapnel. Within a few minutes the floor of the hallway was covered with blood.

The medic had been hit by a piece of metal that had passed completely through his leg without striking bone. It was not a bloody wound, but I could see jerking red muscle in the cut. I tried to give him morphine, but I could not get the needle through the skin. Finally, he took it from me and administered it to himself.

Order of a sort was soon restored and litter bearers were sent for. It was then that I learned that Mac had been hit. He had been standing next to the stove talking to Lt. Ross when a piece of shrapnel had passed through the two wooden walls, striking him in the neck. He lost consciousness almost immediately and Flattery was afraid he would die.

I did not see Mac before he was carried away. I had something more unpleasant to do. I had to return to the platoon on the ridge and tell Crosby. He and Mac had been close friends. Crosby was older; that is, older than most of the rest of us who were in our teens or twenties. Although he tried, he could not keep up with us on marches. We had sought to find him another job, either at company headquarters or farther back, but without success. He and Mac were both devout Catholics and often prayed together.

With another man from the platoon I walked back along the ridge until I found Crosby. "Something's happened to Mac," he said, as soon as he saw my face.

"He got wounded — pretty bad," I said.

Crosby began to whimper and to walk around and around in little circles. "I knew it, I knew it," he kept saying over and over again.

We could neither comfort nor quiet him. Finally, Flattery appeared with orders to move forward again. We left Crosby with Clow, who still had not been picked up by aid men, and moved away toward the edge of the ridge. Neither Crosby nor Clow ever came back to the company.

28

The wet and cold became almost unbearable at our new position. On the way to our position I had been moving about and had been able to keep warm. But sitting on the soggy ground, I grew colder and colder. Finally, I found an excuse to go to the nearby summer house where Flattery and the platoon command group were. There I was able to warm myself for awhile but I could not remain away from the squad long.

When the clouds parted and the sun came out we discovered why the mortar shells had struck near us. High above us on the ridge was what appeared to be a castle. Actually, it was Astenberg, a resort hotel with a high tower which provided observation for miles. Tank destroyers immediately began firing upon it, pounding great holes in its sides. Then the clouds closed over the mountains again and it was lost to view.

After several shivering hours, the second platoon was sent to the I Company left flank. We found it near a road junction. No one there seemed to know why we were there or what we were supposed to do. So we lined up with the end of the I Company flank and squatted under huge pines near a shallow ditch.

By now it was getting dark and soon snow fell, completing the gauntlet of weather through which we had passed that day. After dusk a few German shells shrieked into the woods and exploded. Stiffly, because of the cold, we crawled into the ditch. We were too cold and too tired to dig foxholes.

When the last shell fell everyone got up except Bischoff. He was face down at the bottom of the ditch and wasn't moving. I went over to him and took off his helmet, thinking perhaps he had been hit in the head. I felt his scalp but there was no wound. Then I called a medic over from I Company. "There's nothing I can do for him," he said, "he's got combat fatigue."

After awhile we got Bischoff to his feet, but he would not speak. The only sound he would make was a small whine now and then, like a wounded animal. He kept his arms pressed close to his sides, just as he had placed them under his body when he had dropped to the bottom of the ditch. Two medics finally guided him to a jeep and he was carried away. He never returned to the company.

By now it was dark and bitterly cold. Someone had found some lean-tos nearby, probably made by woodcutters. We crawled into them and huddled close together to keep warm. Flattery had disappeared on a trip to the Company command post. We didn't know what we were supposed to do, so we simply sat, cursed, and tried to sleep, but were unsuccessful because of the cold.

At last, I could stand it no longer. I was angry and I wanted to know what we were supposed to do. "I'm going to find Flattery," I said to Miles McFarland, who had now become a squad leader.

He was too cold to care. "Okay," he said.

The new platoon medic who had been sent up from battalion headquarters was also was trying to find Flattery. He and I set out back down the highway in the snowy night, past the half-track of the morning, now knocked out and shoved to one side of the highway.

We arrived at the big inn of the morning. It was filled with men from I Company and battalion headquarters.

They directed me across the road to the L Company rear command group.

I walked into the door expecting to be dressed down by Madeley, the first sergeant, but to my surprise, he smiled at me and said, "Hi, Heintze, how's it going up there?"

"It's cold," I said.

"Yeah, it's been a pretty rough day," he said.

And suddenly I realized that I was now a full-fledged member of the company. Medeley had accepted me as an equal. I ad come a long way from the first time I had seen this bearded first sergeant (on that first night in the Huertgen Forest) but now I belonged and from now on L Company would always be my company.

Lt. Wheels told me Flattery took his runner and radioman and had gone on up the hill to the castle. No one seemed to regard this as unusual. I thought Flattery should have returned to the platoon. Then Madeley, Lt. Wheels and the rest of the CP rear group got up to leave so I went with them because there seemed nothing else to do.

It was now snowing hard and we could barely see one another in the white darkness. We climbed the hill along the ridge, as we had in the afternoon, and found a road.

Once we took the wrong turn and almost ended in the German lines, but finally we were challenged in front of the castle by a Q sentry from the first platoon.

Inside were prisoners, warmth and Flattery. I found him drying his socks beside a stove.

"What are you doing here?" he said.

"Looking for you," I said.

"Well, as long as you're here, you can go back and get the rest of the platoon."

I shrugged and did not say anything. I left the medic with him, picked up a guide and with him found my way down the hill again to the platoon.

When I arrived most of the men were so cold they could not stand up when I told them we were to move to the hotel. But after massaging their legs for a few minutes, they were able to march back up through the snow to the big cement building. There I fell on a wooden floor beneath a table and slept for four blessed hours.

29

A t 6 o'clock the next morning, we turned the castle-inn over to a company from the 60th Regiment and went back to the road junction where we had been the night before. The ground was covered with snow, frost hung on the barren twigs of the trees and a ghostly fog still filled the air.

Just as we reached the fork in the road, a B-26 bomber, both its motors dead, dipped down out of the fog over our heads. We saw it for only an instant and then it was gone. We waited for the sound it would make as it crashed into the mountains nearby, but it never came Instead, German tanks began firing on the castle-inn in Astenberg, pounding its walls with direct fire, just as our tank destroyers had done the day before.

We moved off, taking the road to the right at the junction to Winterberg. As we advanced, the pines at the left side of the road gradually disappeared and opened on a large deep valley. Then we reached the outskirts of town and were met by a platoon from C Company of the First Battalion. The Germans had departed the day before.

The plan was to follow them by crossing the road, moving into some forest and then out across a wide descending meadow to reach other woods.

With my two scouts I crossed the road and moved through the woods, the rest of the platoon in my wake. But we had hardly emerged to the open field when two mortar shells came in over our heads and exploded behind us. We dashed back to the trees, only to find the rest of the platoon had disappeared.

Finally, we found them in a large house on the other side of the road. Flattery was angry at me for having returned to the woods. He ordered me back to the field again. We looked down the meadow to a small shed in the woods on the other side.

"Run for that," he said.

I did not want to run for it. It was a long way away.

"Come on," he said. "Get the lead out."

I looked at the two scouts and reluctantly got ready to run, but before I could start, another shell came in and exploded in the trees behind us. With that, everyone, including Flatery went back to the house.

We remained there until afternoon and then worked our way back along the highway under the cover of the trees to a point where it was only a short distance to the forest on the other side. I dashed across the road, followed by my squad and then by the entire platoon and the rest of the company. A shell or two exploded some distance away, but we kept moving through the trees along a wood road until it was too dim to see anything. Then we dug shallow holes and went to sleep.

Sometime during the night several shells exploded nearby, breaking the telephone line to the third platoon. Flattery had me wakened to run down the break, something which should have been the runner's job. I cursed and fumed my way until I found it by running the wire through my fingers. It was only a short distance from Flattery's hole. I bound the wire together, said a few choice words and then went back to bed.

Next morning we were pinched out by other units passing in front of us and we returned to Winterberg for a few days in reserve.

30

This, I suppose, is the place to say a few words about Flattery. From this time on until the end of the war, our relations were poor.

The tolerance of men for modern war has no common limit, but 100 days of combat is as good a figure as any. Flattery had seen this much and more. When a man has survived for at least one hundred days in modern warfare, certain things become important, while others drop away.

These things vary, depending on the individual. With Mac and Kosik, self gradually loses its importance. I remember Mac in the last days before he was wounded, becoming less and less interested in what he ate or what he wore. Gradually, he left parts of his excess clothing and equipment behind until he had only a field jacket, a sweater, a rifle, a canteen, a shovel and ammunition.

Flattery was not this kind of a man. He drew to himself over the long passage of combat the need for preservation and comfort. He knew replacements like myself came and went and were unimportant to him individually. He found permanence only in *himself*, he made provision only for *himself* and he believed only in *his* personal ability to survive.

One by one he had seen his friends drop by the wayside, either dead or wounded. One by one he had seen that individual battles were all part of one battle and all existence had become a single long corridor with alternating windows of light and darkness.

Flattery had ability, experience and he wanted to

(and did) survive. But he engendered neither respect nor love. During the last month of the war, he was probably the only competent non-commissioned officer in the company. He could well have been an officer, had he wanted to. He had once, so I was told, been a cook. There also was a rumor he had once been a sheepherder in Montana, his home state, but I think this was untrue.

Flattery was a short heavily built man of 32 who had joined the Third Division in California before the war. He had landed with the Third in North Africa, but before the invasion of Sicily had been transferred to the Ninth to become a rifleman.

He had an unpleasant mushy voice, a round face and a small round mouth. His eyes were pale aid blue and he had a habit of staring fixedly at whomever he was speaking to. In the midst of combat he was fastidious. The final touch to his personality was a small moustache which he always kept immaculately clipped.

I do not often dislike people, but I disliked Flattery very much and he disliked me. He had passed over me in the Rhineland to make Kalman an assistant squad leader. I had never been a squad leader before, but I had wanted to be.

~~~

I felt alone without Mac or Marshall. I had been fighting steadily, I had been wounded once and I was frightened, angry and resentful. I could only blunder along, caught between Flattery's dislike and the necessity to try to stay alive.

Fortunately, after I became a squad leader none of my men were killed or wounded. This was not so much the result of my success in command as it was the nature of the war. By the time we reached Winterberg, the Ruhr Pocket fighting was almost over. It was good to rest, even for a few days. We stayed two days in Winterberg, eating, sleeping and bathing.

On the third day we traveled by truck down a valley to another town whose name I have forgotten and spent the night in some shacks prefabricated by the Todt Organization for slave laborers. The sound of artillery was far away among the hills.

The next day we moved again by truck, winding back and forth through lower and barer hills until, in the late afternoon, we came to Ramsbech.

Here we detrucked and started into the hills again. The entire battalion was soon visible, strung out in a long line in the warm afternoon sun. Eventually we wound up the steep green hillside, a long, hard climb before we reached a crest. We skirted a rock quarry, found some French prisoners of war who had been hiding in the woods and then went down into another valley.

I was thinking how much harder it would be to die on a spring day when a German machine gun began to fire up ahead. Because we were deep in the valley, there was no immediate danger, but the replacements in my squad immediately fell to the ground and looked at me with wonder as I leaned casually against a tree.

After more firing, one of our machine gunners, Meatnose, came limping down the hill with a huge grin on his face. He had been wounded in the fleshy part of the thigh by a machine gun bullet. He was out of it and he knew it, and he was happy.

Then we started forward again, but whatever opposition may have been ahead had disappeared. We walked through groves of trees, dashed across clearings, until, toward evening, we entered a dark wood. At its edge a new valley began. We stopped and set up a defense for the night.

31

I set my guards so they could wake one another beginning at the left side of my part of the line. But early in the morning I woke to find everyone was asleep. Furious, I got everyone up. After some questioning, I found one of the replacements, a reject from the 8th Air Force, had been too frightened to walk to the next man.

As soon as it was light, the second platoon was sent to patrol the woods in the valley below. The memory of that morning always returns to me with pleasure.

We padded silently through the brown woods until we came to a small stream, steaming in the cold morning air. A mist lay over the valley, but as we came out of the woods the sky began to clear and the valley was shot through with sunlight.

We crossed the stream on a small foot bridge, passed a large timbered house, barely visible in the mist, and then, as the sun came out, we were met by a boy riding a bicycle. He told us the German soldiers that were in the valley had all left the night before. As we walked down the valley, he rode ahead of us toward a large farmhouse. We followed, so slowly that he soon disappeared around the corner of a large brown building.

Near the center of the valley, we came across a tiny chapel. Inside was a small altar and six pews. We moved on to the farmhouse and searched it. It was a huge place, three stories tall and seemed to be filled with endless numbers of civilians.

The lady of the house fried us some potatoes. We sat and ate them in the courtyard, and drank fresh milk, the first we had had in months.

A Polish prisoner, still in his Polish army uniform, talked to us as we sat and waited for the rest of the company to appear. He had worked at the farm and told us he knew where a German artillery battery was hidden in the woods. We doubted his story.

The rest of the company came down off the hill and entered another group of buildings farther up the valley. My squad was ordered to patrol in front of this position. The mist had disappeared completely by now and we strolled along in the warm sunlight, and gradually climbed a road until we came to the place where it intersected with another highway.

There was a house at the intersection and in front of the house an old man aid his two grandchildren sat on benches. We sat beside them, talked and gave the children candy from our rations. Like the boy on the bicycle, he said German troops had been in the valley the night before, but they had left at dawn.

After awhile, Captain Heater of M Company drove up in a jeep, followed by five jeeps from his company. I showed them the road from which we had come. He suggested we hitch a ride back to the farmhouse. There we sat dozing in the sun for an hour. Then the company formed up and began to hike toward the open end of the valley.

After a short walk, we came to a larger village, occupied by the rest of the battalion. We were ordered to set up a roadblock at the edge of town and had just commandeered a bedroom when we were displaced by a captain from battalion headquarters. But he had no chance to use it. In half an hour, we moved forward again, toward another village 3,000 yards away.

We never reached it. Before we had gone a mile, we

were halted at another large collection of buildings. The Fifth Division had crossed in front of us. The battle for the Ruhr Pocket was over.

32

Our stop at the large farm lasted for three days. We slept at night in a large barn, making our beds in a bin of chaff. The second day we were there, training began.

At night, we outposted the village in all directions. During the day I talked with a young Russian slave laborer, a well indoctrinated Communist who tried hard to convert us to his cause. He was intensely happy and managed to smile his way into our chow line every day.

More replacements came into the platoon. They all seemed new and alien. I felt like an old man who has lived beyond his time. I realized I was the only man here of the 29 who had entered combat on Oct. 13 of the year before. One of the group was now a cook's helper, one was a machine gunner, but I was the only one still in a rifle platoon.

All of the us had been wounded and some had been killed. Of the group who had come into combat the following day, the group that included Marshall, only one, Miles McFarland, now a squad leader, had come this far without being wounded.

On our third day at the farm, we boarded trucks and drove 160 miles toward the center of Germany, traveling from the Westerwald and Sauerland to the plains before the Harz Momtains. I don't remember most of the journey except catching a glimpse of a trainload of V-2 rockets somewhere and Nordhausen.

Nordhausen had been almost completely destroyed by a bombing raid, but just beyond it was a concentration camp. As we passed hundreds of its dead were being buried in long ditches.

We stopped for the night at Rotha and spent the night in a barn, sleeping behind the house of a man whose wife and children had been killed by American bombs. He could not conceal his hatred of us.

Next morning we started into the Harz Mountains. The sky was overcast and we walked along dirt roads for 12 miles without meeting any opposition. The day was chiefly noticeable because of the irregular, killing pace we maintained. Lt. Ross was still commanding the company and he stopped frequently to consult his map. Every time he stopped the company jerked to a halt.

In the evening we stopped at Rohrbach, one of many towns in Germany with such a name and stayed in a house with a widow and her two small children. She was very frightened. Her son hung an airplane model from the kitchen ceiling and she thought this angered us. She ordered him to take it down, although it did not matter to us.

Next day we marched off, but this time I led the company and the pace was far more even. We were the reserve company of the battalion and we followed the rear of K Company through low rolling hills. It was a lovely day, the sun shone, the grass was green, the trees had begun to leaf out and farmers were out plowing the fields, oblivious of war.

We passed through several small villages where no one had even bothered to hang out white flags. Once we came across an abandoned road block of felled trees.

In the afternoon we came to a pretty village with a cafe that had set tables cut under the trees. We sent scouts out to search the place first, but they found it already occupied by troops of the 104th Division.

For the rest of the day we waited for transportation. The division was now spread thinly over miles of the Harz Mountains and it was difficult to provide trucks. Late in the afternoon the 26th Field Artillery arrived and we climbed on their trucks and drove until it was almost dark.

Most of the towns we passed had already been overrun by armored divisions. We could see their chalked route signs, usually the word "tanks" followed by an arrow or a copy of military government regulations pasted on a wall. But we seldom saw other Americans.

After supper, we received orders to attack Alsleben, a town on the bank of the Saale River. A patrol from B Company had entered it that night and had been fired upon.

We spent most of the night trying to find a place to sleep. We were to attack at 3 o'clock in the morning, but it was 11 o'clock before we could find a house in which to lie down. I woke feeling I had not really slept at all.

33

The road to Alsleben ran across a plain as flat and level as Kansas. We trudged along it for three miles and arrived at the edge of Alsleben just as it was beginning to dawn.

In one of the first houses, we found an old, badly frightened couple. They told us soldiers had been in their house the afternoon before. We assumed the Germans had moved on, as they had been doing for several weeks and we moved confidentially toward the center of the city.

The street soon branched into two more streets. Without pausing, we took the street to the right. A high wall ran along its left side. At the end of the street in the half-light of dawn, the first scout of Marchek's squad collided with a German non-commissioned officer.

He had his machine pistol slung over his shoulder. Before he could swing it around into a firing position, he and the scout began to wrestle with one another. The German bit the scout's finger. The scout took off his helmet and beat the German into unconsciousness. Then we dragged him into a nearby cellar and turned him over to the German family living there.

When we returned to the street, we could see more Germans passing the corner ahead. Hurriedly, we ran to the shelter of a doorway and found ourselves in a kind of courtyard made by the walls of three barns and the house. Three men from Marchek's squad remained on the street, potting away at the street corner without hitting anyone.

Flattery ordered me to retrace our steps to the first street intersection and investigate the street above us. It stood slightly higher than the courtyard where the rest of the platoon had taken shelter.

I did not find any other Americans. They had moved to the right toward the river and we had lost contact with them. A search up the street produced only a number of frightened German civilians. We returned to the courtyard.

I went upstairs in the house and stood by a dormer window, looking out, but I didn't see anything.

Flattery moved some of the platoon to the largest barn across the courtyard. Through its windows, one could look out on a church graveyard and a high wall. Most of the men in the barn were from my squad so I joined them.

A new company runner walked to use an outhouse at the edge of the barnyard. When he had finished, he stepped out and was shot in the chest. We could hear him through the barn door calling for help. Our new platoon medic, Bell, stepped out to give him first aid. He, too, was shot.

The two men lay together, now both crying for assistance. Flattery peaked at them through the barn door, but he would not let anyone go to their aid. Clearly, the Germans had filtered down the street from where I had just come and were firing from the higher ground at anything that moved.

In the barn Wagner looked out one of the windows and then said, "Are there any GI's out there?"

"Hell, no," Flattery said.

191

He crept to the wall and peeked out the window just in time to see the gray figure of a German soldier slither over the wall and drop into the churchyard. He pushed Wagner aside and fired his machine pistol. The German did not get up. Tamen, who was at the other window, fired twice killing a man who had already crossed the wall.

I sat in a bin of chaff through all this, listening to the platoon radio. The radio had been picking up German voices, but I could not understand them, except for *"durch, durch, durch!" Through, through, through!*

At last I gave up and went to one of the windows to join in watching the churchyard wall. For a long time it was silent. The wind tossed the leaves in the graveyard, the sun shone. We waited and waited. Unknown to us, the first and third platoons also had met the enemy. Their situation was no better than ours.

We had collided with a company of SS troops moving south out of the Harz Mountains. Some of SS had crawled to the house where the first platoon had taken shelter and had called for them to surrender. The third platoon's medical aid man had been killed and Bill Harlan, my friend of beachhead days, had been wounded in both legs.

Suddenly there was a flash, a roar and a panzerfaust shell tore through a kind of cupelo above us without doing damage. We all retreated momentarily from the windows, but Flattery drove us back.

We sat in the barn for a long time, unable to get either in or out while outside the cries of the wounded men grew weaker and weaker and finally stopped completely. They were both dead.

Then as suddenly as it had begun the situation reversed itself. The third platoon cut up the cross street ahead of us and isolated the SS platoon. A brave German civilian walked down the street to the house where they were holed up had talked eighteen of them into surrendering.

Freed from the barn, we dashed across the courtyard, avoiding a look at the two bodies lying there, went back around the church and up the street in the direction of the attack. My squad led the way and I led the squad, dashing from one house to the next along a row of small buildings. The houses were wall to wall and the SS had moved along them by climbing over the backyard fences.

Halfway down the street I thundered into a front hallway to meet a young SS trooper face to face. His hands were clasped over his head and on a chair near the door he had neatly piled his machine pistol, his own personal 38 caliber police pistol and a panzerfaust. I grabbed the pistol and ordered him outside.

We came to a corner to find the cross street ran to the north for half a mile until it disappeared in the open plain beyond. Both sides of the street were lined with houses. We began searching them, but we soon found they were empty of soldiers.

Halfway up the street we found a jeep from the 26th Field Artillery and out of it sprawled the figure of a dead American. The jeep had been ambushed the night before.

When we reached the edge of town, we saw a large farmhouse a quarter of a mile farther down the highway. Flattery sent me to outpost it. It was a huge complex of buildings and barns. We had just settled down

193

to rest when a battalion anti-tank gun crew appeared. They had been ordered to take over the position.

Wearily, we moved back to town to find it filled with marauding Polish and Russian slave laborers. They had broken into a liquor store and now drunk, they were careening through the streets on horses and in wagons. We did nothing to interfere and instead looked for a place to sleep.

Half my squad ended up in a bakery where they were treated to freshly baked bread. The other half slept in the bedroom of the house next door. Once again the Air Force rejects slept through their guard duty.

For this action, Flattery received the Silver Star, but most of us remembered it because of the death of Bell and Angelo and Flattery's unwillingness to allow us to try to help them.

34

The next morning we climbed aboard any transportation we could find and rode away from the river to the northeast, searching for SS. The land was low with a few trees and villages. We passed collections of barns and went up and down over small hills. At the top of one hill we saw several towns in the distance, one of them surrounded a factory with a tall smoking smokestack.

It was again a bright, sunny day and it seemed inappropriate to have to fight a war. We had begun the day on the half-tracks of the battalion antitank guns. A mile from the first village, the column halted and for the first and only time during my service, the antitank guns were unlimbered and fired.

Someone professed to have seen a tank. The first round was one hundred yards wide of this target. It hit a house. The second shot hit and set afire the "tank," that on closer inspection proved to be a tractor standing unattended in a field.

We walked the rest of the distance to the village to find it contained a German replacement company, stranded there without transportation. It was composed of reservists in their 30s. They had been sitting philosophically in a large barn waiting for us to appear. They seemed very happy to surrender.

We searched the rest of the town, confiscating all the foiling pieces from the gun case of a large landowner and then were driven to another nearby village to spend the night. I took four men and slept in the house of the local police chief who was afraid he would be assassinated by slave laborers without such protection.

35

Next morning we started late, marching off across the flat country along a road lined with trees and walls. We had not gone far, however, when we heard tanks behind us and a squadron of the 4th Cavalry Group rolled up.

After a short conference between commanding officers, we all were loaded aboard their new light M-26 tanks and set out across the open country. The only bad feature of the new vehicles was their exhaust which opened upward behind the turret where we were standing. Our feet were soon warm and my poncho ended the day with a hole singed through it.

The cavalry reconn troop, all jeeps and armored cars, raced along the flanks, moving to the height of land. We could seem them against the horizon. After a few miles, we reached the crest of a low hill and saw another village below us. The recon jeeps and arnored cars had already entered the village and were prowling about its streets.

Overhead an artillery spotting plane buzzed back and forth. Soon the cub landed and the two officers aboard climbed out and came over to talk to us. They had watched the entry of the recon troop and tanks bearing the first platoon.

"We saw a couple of Germans duck around the corner and into a cellar," the observer said. "Gee, I wish we could have gotten word to you."

The town yielded a second replacement company, also stranded. They had no weapons and so surrendered without firing a shot.

The column of vehicles moved out again. We swept through th village under the limbs of leafing trees, past frightened Germans out into the open country beyond, aware for the first time of how the armored infantry must have fought the war.

Half an hour later we were in another village. White flags hung from every window. We did not pause, but roared through it on down the macadam highway. Ahead the valley broadened and lengthened. At the far end we could see a large city.

The flank patrols moved to the hills. One of them flushed a deer, but it got away before they could kill it. Before long they were on high ground overlooking the city of Quedlinberg. There they halted and the column stopped, too. There was a long wait. We climbed down from the tanks and sunned ourselves.

At length the squadron's assault guns wheeled up, put out aiming stakes and began firing, filling the afternoon stillness with hollow bangs. Then the tanks moved forward, leaving us behind. Soon we could hear heavy firing from the direction of Quedlinberg.

Another half hour passed. The tanks returned and we climbed aboard and raced toward town over plowed fields. The sound of firing was still intense as we unloaded under trees near the edge of the city and walked to the first house. We did not see return fire, but the cavalry blazed away. Someone had fired on the recon troop and tanks were using both their cannon and machine guns to reply.

By now it was dusk. We moved on in the darkness, searching out a few houses without finding anything. Just as it got completely dark we came to a river. A bridge spanned it, leading into the central part of the city.

"Get across and into the first house on the right," Flattery said to me.

I looked doubtfully at the bridge. It was bare of cover and it appeared to be about 130 yards to the house. I got ready to make the dash, when one of the tank crews strolled up and walked to the center of the bridge. There they fired several shots in the direction of the city.

"I thought I saw somebody down the street," one of them said to me as I ran past.

We found the first house filled with people, most of them in the cellar. Beyond was a large courtyard and the dark shapes of barns. I sent my men to search them and then looked through the house. Upstairs was empty, but at the head of the cellar stairs I found the owner. He assured me it was empty of German soldiers.

In a moment the rest of the platoon appeared and then two tanks rumbled across the bridge and parked outside on the street. They were followed by two jeeps from M Company.

Flattery ordered me to move to the next house up the street. I had just started forward when a small Opel sedan without lights came racing down the street toward us. Both M Company machine guns opened fire. The lights of the car came on and the car came to a screeching halt. Everyone began yelling "Cease fire, cease fire!" but it was a moment before the machine guns stopped.

Inside the car were a doctor, a nurse, a woman and her small child. The doctor's leg had almost been severed, the nurse had three bullets in her and the woman, a heart patient they had been taking to the hospital, had fainted. She died a few minutes later.

After order had been restored and the wounded had

been carried away, I moved on to the next house where we stopped for the night.

I had just placed a guard at the gate and gone upstairs when a woman appeared from the darkness. She was on her way to her sister's house, a block or two away — or so she said. I guided her there.

When I returned to the house, I found two girls and a boy who had been hiding in the cellar. They, too, wanted an escort back across the river. So I took them to their house.

Back at the house, I found one of the men in McFarland's squad across the street had killed a German paratrooper who had appeared from somewhere. That was the last incident of the night.

I went upstairs and fell asleep.

36

At daybreak the next morning we started into town, searching houses as we went. For some distance we found no one. Eventually, we stopped searching because the houses were all three or four stories high and it was a long climb to their top floors.

In one narrow street near the cathedral, we flushed out a medical officer, accompanied by a pretty woman who kept screaming at us, "This is a free city, why did you fire?"

It developed that the burgermeister of Quedlinberg and the town commander had disagreed over what should be done about the resistance the day before. The mayor wanted Quedlinberg declared a free city. The town commander felt it his duty to offer at least token resistance. The few shots his men had fired had brought down the artillery of the cavalry which had inflicted some minor damage.

The medical officer had a pistol and refused to surrender it, even though, by terms of the Geneva Convention, he was not supposed to be armed. He complained so angrily that Lt. Cohen, the cavalry troop commander, finally took it away by force and ordered the officer to march with his hands over his head in front of a tank to the center of town.

There we found a barracks, abandoned by the troops defending the town. They had fled to the hills in the distance. Lt. Cohen found a pile of old rifles in the barracks. He laid them on a street corner curb and then ran over them with his tank, mashing and twisting their barrels beyond use.

The town cleared, we sat down in the sun against a wooden fence and talked to several young boys who had appeared from somewhere. One of them was an expert on tanks and held a learned conversation with me on the merits and demerits of Sherman and Tiger tanks.

At last, we left our tanker friends and walked to the far edge of town to take cover in a small house with two women who had been bombed out of Berlin. While we watched hungrily, they ate a thick soup. They did not offer to share it with us.

Later we were sent to search a hill beyond the city. It was a warm spring day — it was almost May — and we climbed slowly upward over terraces of vegetables. At the top of the hill, we found an air raid warning tower. One of my men climbed to its observation deck, tore out the telephone inside and hurled it to the ground.

Farther on, we came to a cave cleverly painted green to blend with the hillside. Inside were rows and rows of benches which marked it as an air raid shelter. Beyond its entrance we crept to within a few feet of a woman and her children. They never heard us or knew that we were watching them.

The whole hill, we found with further exploration, was hollow. It once had been a wine cellar, but had been converted into a mass air raid shelter. We entered near the top of the hill and wandered down through its galleries until we emerged at a lower exit.

At last we returned to the town having found what we had sought — nothing.

Flattery was waiting for us. The rest of the platoon had already moved to the southern part of the city. At first we were billeted in a schoolhouse, but later moved to the upper floors of three-story apartment houses.

Quedlinberg was anything but docile in occupation. That night shots were fired at our men and I Company was ordered to make a regular nightly patrol of the streets.

The next morning a boy tossed a grenade into a shower tent set up by the river (fortunately no one was injured) and that afternoon a mine was exploded in an empty air raid shelter not far away.

The next day I talked to an attractive widow with two small children who lived in the apartment house. Her husband had been killed in Russia. She showed me a pamphlet about England and the United States and tried to tell me she understood why other countries made war on Germany. She would have been in her late teens when Hitler came to power, I thought, and had lived through the post World War I inflation and the unrest of the early 1930s.

I tried to argue with her, but next morning she told me "peopled had warned her to stop talking to soldiers." Until that moment the power of the totalitarian state we were fighting had been something I had read about, but did not really know.

I have often wondered about that woman for later Quedlinberg became a part of East Germany. But I suppose I will never know how she experienced that regime.

37

That same day Flattery assigned my squad to relieve a battalion section that had been guarding a wholesale grocery warehouse not far away. It was a two-story brick building filled with matches, canned goods, biscuits and other staples. Russians from a nearby slave labor camp had broken into it and looted it. The owners one Eric Meyer, had requested a guard.

The battalion section guarding it left before we arrived. When we reached the building we found it full of Russians and Poles, helping themselves to food. I drove them back out into the street, but they stood before the door begging for "just a little marmalade."

Shortly afterward Meyer, a fat, jolly German in a fine overcoat, manicured nails, and a spotless hat appeared. He inspected the building, clicking his tongue, shaking his head and occasionally smiling at me. With him was a woman in her 20's who greeted me with "How's everything, pal? Okay?"

Her story was that she had returned to Germany from Brooklyn just before the beginning of the war and had been unable to return home. She made a special point of asking that I be sure the slave laborers not steal Meyer's bicycle.

We spent the night in the warehouse. The Russians and Poles circled around the door, but we ignored them and eventually they returned to their camp.

At noon the next lay Flattery came for an inspection tour and said he thought we might be moving on later that day, but it seemed unlikely.

After lunch Bruner and two other men from my squad, Grouse and Junior, the last one of the Air Force misfits, asked if they could visit the slave labor camp. Grouse, it turned out, had already done so. On his return he had tempted the other two with tales of beautiful eager women and large quantities of beer and schnapps.

"Okay," I said. "But be back in an hour."

They had hardly disappeared when the platoon runner, Pelky, arrived at the warehouse.

"We're moving out in half an hour,' he reported.

I sent another man after the missing and rounded up the remainder of the squad. When we reached the rest of the platoon, I was roundly chewed out by Flattery — with good reason. Fortunately for me, my missing men arrived before we departed.

38

We left Quedlinberg in a convoy of captured German trucks. Their drivers had surrendered and offered to place both themselves and their vehicles at the disposal of their captors. Because the division was short both on gas and transportation, the offer was accepted and the strange convoy of creaking German trucks loaded with American soldiers wound up into the Harz Mountains the rest of the day.

We were sent into the woods to sweep them. The remains of an SS army was supposed to be in the area and it was our job to find them and bring them in as prisoners.

Our base of operations was Guntersberg, a large village not far from the Brocken. Each morning we formed up there, walked into the woods, reformed in a skirmish line and moved through the trees until we came to another village.

The work was neither very dangerous, nor very rewarding. During the three or four days we were at it, we turned up only about a dozen prisoners. We passed through a variety of woods, tall majestic pines, small trees so close together we almost could not pass, rolling open hills and hardwoods.

Almost every night we returned to Guntersberg and to the same house. It was run by a huge German woman we all called Momma. She was the kindest person we had met. Each night when we returned to the village, she would welcome us, make us sleep in her bedroom, give us food, heat us water for coffee and made us feel as if we were her sons.

The house was really not hers. It belonged to her daughter. Her daughter's husband had been lost at sea aboard a submarine and the daughter had taken up with a Yugoslav soldier who worked her land. Momma also was caring for an orphan boy, Karl. In the meantime, she had no idea what had happened to her own home in another village nearby.

After three days of hikes through the woods, we left Guntersberg and one bright sunny morning passed out of the mountains and crossed the plain between Halle and Leipzig to the city of Dessau.

39

Dessau was a moderately famous city. It was the home of the Bauhaus and also a Junkers factory where Stuka dive bombers had once been built. Because of the aircraft factory it had been heavily bombed. Two raids, one a great fire raid by the Royal Air Force had razed the whole center of the city. There almost nothing remained except the shells of the buildings.

We rode through the rubble cluttered streets, dodging broken street car cables curled in the mortar dust and broken bricks. We passed the modern city hall, an ugly block of green cement, pocked with bullet holes, saw signs that warned looters they would be shot on sight, scrawled chalked notes telling sadly of other addresses where former occupants could be found and noted large concrete water tanks spaced regularly along the sidewalks to fight incendiaries. In the end they had proved useless in preventing the destruction of the city.

Only a few walked the streets. Although the sun shone, a dead air hung over everything, a feeling of foreboding, ruin and despair.

We unloaded and walked to the Mulde River bank to relieve the Third Armored Division. It had captured the city after a hard fight with fanatic Hitler youth armed with panzerfausts.

As we searched for the Third Armored's command post, a single shell from the American side rocketed over the river and crashed in Rosslau, a suburb still in German hands.

We were assigned a platoon front of almost a mile.

We could do so only by setting up three outposts and by patrolling regularly between them. The first and most northerly outpost was in a house beside a broken wooden footbridge. The second was a quarter of a mile away at a cement bridge which had been blown up. Its span now lay in the Mulde. It was still possible to cross the river here by walking on what still remained of the bridge.

The third outpost lay around a bend in the river further upstream. Once a pontoon bridge had been anchored there to permit a crossing to a park on the east bank of the river, but it, too, had been destroyed.

This was my squad's responsibility. We moved into an apartment house across the street from the river, one of two buildings in the block still standing. A German family lived on the first, second and third floors. The fourth floor was empty.

We ousted the Germans and took over the entire building. There were seven of us. Each of us had his own room. The first floor had once been a store, but had been converted into an office for the motorcycle branch of the Nazi Party.

Because of the patrols required between the outposts, we were up most of the night. We patrolled to the main cement bridge. The first squad patrolled to it from the other direction.

Almost from the first day we arrived, it was clear there would be no fire from the other side of the river. On the second day a platoon from I Company crossed the bridge and patrolled to the limit of their radio's range. They found only one prisoner, a motorcycle courier.

Instead of fighting our chief problem soon became

one of keeping the German civilians on the other side of the river from crossing to the west bank. The Mulde joined the Elbe just north of Dessau. Together they marked the limit of the American advance. Here we were to wait the arrival of the Russians. As they moved toward us, they squeezed the Germans, both soldiers and civilians toward us.

In a few days the first German soldiers began appearing at the cement bridge. Under huge packs they clambered over the broken slabs of the span. First there was only a trickle of men, then a stream and finally a torrent.

Whole companies marched across it to surrender, battalions of antiaircraft batteries, infantry, reservists, wounded and convalescing SS troopers, Luftwaffe and Wehrmacht Hilfe girls, hundreds, then thousands, seeking to escape Soviet troops. Extra men from battalion and division headquarters had to be sent up to help handle the load.

Once they surrendered and crossed the bridge, the Germans were loaded fifty to a semi-truck and trailer and hauled back to prisoner of war cages. Then slowly the flood began to diminish and finally it stopped completely.

Next British and American prisoners of war appeared. Most were from a large camp at Luckenwalde, 103 kilometers to the east. The Russians had surrounded the camp, but they were not eager to release the prisoners. The Americans and British tired of waiting and slipped over the camp fences. Then they either walked or hitched a ride to the bridge. Some had been prisoners for as long as five years. They seemed dazed and unable to believe they finally were free.

Then this traffic, too, ended, and German civilians began to appear along the riverbank. We had been ordered to keep them all on their side of the river, but many crossed anyway. Some swam. Women sold themselves or their favors to American soldiers. Women, in general, became an increasing problem. Dessau was full of them and they were starved for male companionship. Non-fraternization was supposed to be in force, but it stopped at nightfall.

Despite the traffic in prisoners, we kept the patrols up at night. I always enjoyed the walk and I made it so many times I could almost do it in my sleep.

From our house, we crossed the street, dodged between two buildings which were only shells and emerged at the river bank. Usually the moon was shining. It made the water in the mill race pond behind a dam downstream a milky white. Across the stream stood the black and broken trees of the park.

We would walk rapidly past the machine gun holes carefully dug in the west bank and marked with stakes and ranges — how ironic they were pointing toward all that remained of Germany, nothing in either direction.

We passed through what had once been an open air cafe, moved along the high wall of a four-story black and gutted museum, crossed the mill race, went past its broken and rusting wheel and the still smoldering wheat in the mill, through a dark passage and came out on the bridge approach where the guards of McFarland's squad stood.

Behind us the town was still. Only the white water gushing through the broken stones of the bridge and the wind in the trees of the park made any sound.

Walking that path was penetrating to the end of war — nothingness.

We stood in awe of what had happened, we walked carefully, as one walks with the ghosts near a cemetery, afraid to wake the dead. And there, at the edge of what had once been form and substance, life and a city, where once men had lived together in peace and had grown, with their buildings, old, and where one mad day they had surrendered all of this, the war ended.

That May evening we sat in the office of the apartment beside the stove drinking coffee and listening to the celebration of VE Day in London. Outside it was quiet. There was nothing to say.

Only, I remember, I went to the window and pulled up the blackout blinds. Through the window I could see the stars.

POSTSCRIPT

San Jose, March to May, 1952

For those who are interested in sequels, I came home in 1946 after a stay in the Army of Occupation.

Flattery left Germany soon after V-E Day. Our differences had, by that time, been resolved into a wary kind of truce. I do not know what happened to him.

Madeley, the first sergeant, left the company in Dessau, but he could not stay away from the army. In 1946, shortly after I left the company, he returned to it to again be the first sergeant.

Mac lived, although disabled, married and lives in Chicago.

Buck Miller was first a newspaper reporter and then a public relations man in Pennsylvania.

Miles McFarland became a pharmacist in Columbus, Ohio.

Kiser was killed in an automobile accident in the Middle West shortly after the war.

Lt. Ross became a National Guard instructor.

Lt. Wheels remained in the army and eventually became a colonel.

Marshall received his commission as a second lieutenant after he returned to the United States to recover from his wounds. He volunteered for additional duty and spent a year in Bremen. Then he returned to civilian life, became a college professor, was recalled to duty in the Korean War and spent a year in Korea before returning to Illinois to teach.

The others also have gone, each on their separate way and now share with me only the memory of the time when we wore the same uniform, endured the same hardships, felt the same fears and knew the same joys and disappointments.

Yet as I sit here in California, I wonder if they, as I, still occasionally remember those days when we were young and when we forged the shape of victory. In the chaos of our age for a brief moment we stood at its center and saw events become history and caught for a moment a glimpse of what we might have become.

And I wonder if they, as I, ask: Why did we fight?

There can be no simple, single answer.

We fought because we had to. In the fragmentary and futile efforts most of us make to shape our own lives, we never really plan our future.

We ignored, for as long as we were able, direct involvement in war. When it finally came one Sunday morning, like a bad dream, we waked to find it about us. We reached its outer edge without ever having really understood it. Before we could pause, we were a part of it, vastly involved in its mechanics.

For it was, above all, a mechanical war. We discovered, perhaps without understanding it at first, that it could be won by materiel and machines. It fascinated us. It was a great contrivance for which we had only to construct the proper parts. After that it worked by itself.

It was seldom a crusade. Often it was a job. We found rules to follow, patterns in which to fit, habits to learn, a vast and impersonal machinery to build.

It was a modern war, the product of a civilization in

which technique has come to replace human relationships. We did not need so much to be taught the reason for fighting, as we had to learn the way to bring destructive power to bear on our enemies.

It was a total effort. It demanded unquestioning loyalty and allegiance. To fight was to perform an act of faith. To perform that act of faith required a surrender of the will. Once this had been done, it was possible only to question one's faith.

It was a patriotic war, but it was not compounded of a great love for flags, the Constitution or similar symbols. It was a fight without slogans and songs. Instead our patriotism was inarticulate and we were an armed force which yearned for home and family. We went out to strange places and to greatly unequal experiences: coral atolls, jungles, arctic islands, London, Paris, Rome, the farm lands of half a dozen countries and we saw them all as tourists and did not understand them.

It was a war in which we seldom hated the enemy. How can one hate a foe he does not see except as the broken shape of a human body or the degraded despair of a prisoner. Instead our hate was spent on our superiors, on the minor pin pricks of military existence which magnify themselves in the tension of conflict.

Because it was a total war, we fought for survival, knowing that if we lost, we would end, as our enemies did, in complete surrender. We believed what was at stake was a somewhat uncertain collection of beliefs vaguely defined as "the American way of life." Perhaps we thought this was the right to be left alone, even though this happy freak of historical chance would never again come to us.

Finally, we fought because we felt that human bond

CPSIA information can be obtained
at www.ICGtesting.com
Printed in the USA
FFOW05n0048050414

without which we could never have built a single unit of fighting men. It was a simple loyalty to others. We wanted our squad, platoon or company to be the best. We wanted to fight well. We wanted to do the job right.

So, for better or worse, without asking anything except to be allowed to return to a dream we had never fully realized and would never find, we performed an act of faith and surrendered ourselves, each of us as he was able, to the challenge of war, that state which is at once the most exalted and most depraved condition of human existence.

And then peace came, or such peace as any of us was ever to know and we relaxed into lives which turned not on outposts and orders nor upon the harsh commands of sergeants and lieutenants. We now grow older in a new conflict which is both a continuation of the old and something quite different. It colors all that we see of it. To it there is no decision, no victory and no end. And perhaps we forget.

And yet, for most of us, war will always mean this: a time when we were young and of a band, when we, above all else, were riflemen, basic, 745's.